DEVELOPING ENGLISH TEACHERS

Open University Press

English, Language, and Education series

General Editor: Anthony Adams
Lecturer in Education, University of
Cambridge

SELECTED TITLES IN THE SERIES

The Problem with Poetry
Richard Andrews

Writing Development
Roslyn Arnold

Simulations in English Teaching
Paul Bambrough

Writing Policy in Action
Eve Bearne and Cath Farrow

Secondary Worlds
Michael Benton

Thinking Through English
Paddy Creber

Teaching Secondary English
David Curtis

What is English Teaching?
Chris Davies

Developing English
Peter Dougill (ed.)

**The Primary Language Book (2nd
Edition)**
Peter Dougill

Reading Against Racism
Emrys Evans (ed.)

Developing English Teachers
Andrew Goodwyn

English Teaching and Media Education
Andrew Goodwyn

English at the Core
Peter Griffith

Literary Theory and English Teaching
Peter Griffith

**Lesbian and Gay Issues in the English
Classroom**
Simon Harris

Reading and Response
Mike Hayhoe and Stephen Parker (eds)

Reassessing Language and Literacy
Mike Hayhoe and Stephen Parker (eds)

Who Owns English?
Mike Hayhoe and Stephen Parker (eds)

Language and the English Curriculum
John Keen

Shakespeare in the Classroom
Susan Leach

Developing Readers in the Middle Years
Elaine Millard

Language Awareness for Teachers
Bill Mittins

The Making of English Teachers
Robert Protherough and Judith Atkinson

Young People Reading
Charles Sarland

Learning About Language
Alison Sealey

School Writing
Yanina Sheeran and Douglas Barnes

Playing the Language Game
Valerie Shepherd

Reading Narrative as Literature
Andrew Stibbs

**Reading Within and Beyond the
Classroom**
Dan Taverner

Reading for Real
Barrie Wade (ed.)

Spoken English Illuminated
Andrew Wilkinson, Alan Davies and
Deborah Berrill

DEVELOPING ENGLISH TEACHERS

The role of mentorship in a reflective profession

Andrew Goodwyn

Open University Press
Buckingham · Philadelphia

Open University Press
Celtic Court
22 Ballmoor
Buckingham
MK18 1XW

and
1900 Frost Road, Suite 101
Bristol, PA 19007, USA

First Published 1997

A catalogue record of this book is available from the British Library

ISBN 0 335 19760 4 (pb)

Library of Congress Cataloging-in-Publication Data
Goodwyn, Andrew, 1954–
    Developing English teachers : the role of mentorship in a
reflective profession / Andrew Goodwyn.
        p.   cm.
    Includes bibliographical references and index.
    ISBN 0–335–19760–4 (pb)
    1. English philosophy—Study and teaching—Theory, etc. 2. English
teachers—Training of.   3. Mentorship.   I. Title.
PE66.G66   1997
428'.007—dc21   96–53331
                                                                      CIP

Typeset by Graphicraft Typesetters Ltd., Hong Kong
Printed in Great Britain by St Edmundsbury Press, Bury St Edmunds, Suffolk

Dedication

It seems especially appropriate to dedicate this book on developing English teachers to three important figures from the world of English teaching and from teacher education in particular, figures who have certainly been mentors to me, and many others, over their distinguished careers.

Anthony Adams for his personal help and support and for his unfailing efforts to keep English teachers up to date and facing the future with excitement and commitment, one of the most significant aspects of his work being the excellent series of books of which this is a modest example.

Robert Protherough for his generous help and advice and in recognition of his superlative contribution, through his many and varied writings, to all aspects of thinking about English teaching.

Desmond Vowles for his constant and clear-sighted advice and counsel, his prevailing kindness and principled generosity and, as my own, original, supervisor, for setting me off down that particular English teacher's path.

I hope they will think that, for others undertaking a similar journey, this book may be a small, but useful, signpost.

Contents

Acknowledgements   viii
General editor's introduction   ix

Introduction   1
1   The potential of partnership: mentors and school-based
    initial teacher education   5
2   Coming to terms with 'English': student teachers,
    mentors and the subject of English   26
3   Becoming a mentor: managing the learning of student
    teachers of English   48
4   Being the mentor: looking after the learning of student
    teachers of English   70
5   Developing new English teachers: managing the
    transition into the profession   91
6   Developing ourselves: English teachers and continuous
    professional development   115

Notes   138
Bibliography   143
Index   147

Acknowledgements

I should like to acknowledge the help of all the English teachers with whom I have worked over the years, who have helped me to begin to understand the role of the mentor.

I should like to acknowledge the help and support of my many colleagues on the PGCE course at Reading University, and in particular James Hall and Keith Postlethwaite, principal architects of partnership, who directed the course for three incredibly demanding and highly productive years.

I should like to say thank you to the group who have worked and continue to work with me on the ACE (Advanced Certificate in the teaching of English) project: Elaine Murray, Winston Brookes, Ken Bush, Theresa Dawes, Jane Everton, Jenny Hastings, Rick Holroyd, Ron Middleton, Heather Owens and Pete Rowe. I should especially like to thank Mike Harrison as the main collaborator on the project for his determined commitment and his unfailing good humour.

Finally, I should like to thank Anne Wilstead, for reading and improving the text, for liking some of its stories and for her love and support.

General editor's introduction

Readers in England and Wales will be only too well aware of the changes that are taking place in initial teacher education; those elsewhere may like to know that most of the time in initial teacher education or 'training' as it is now being called, is spent in schools rather than in an institution of higher education. Thus the task of preparing the new teacher for the classroom falls increasingly and more extensively on the teachers in the schools, generally known as 'mentors'. The crucial idea is that of 'partnership', with schools and higher education institutions (HEIs) working ever more closely together.

These changes have not met with altogether universal approval. I have frequently expressed reservations about the direction that events are taking in this respect and it is certainly the case that many schools and teachers are finding the task of mentoring a further demand upon people whose professional life is already overcrowded. In Northern Ireland, for example, the move towards greater school involvement in the training process has been resisted by the schools themselves and the pattern of initial teacher education has remained of a much more traditional kind. In Scotland, too, things have moved in a much less extreme way than in England and Wales. Even in Cambridge, where there has traditionally been a very close link between the Department of Education in the university and English departments in the schools, the signs of strains developing under the new patterns of work are already beginning to show.

There are many different patterns of both partnership and mentoring beginning to develop and the present volume explores a number of these, including that operating at the author's own university of Reading, so as to critically appraise good and bad models of the mentoring process.

Some of us feel that there are real problems in the diminution of the role of the HEIs in the initial stages of preparing new teachers for the classroom, not least a potential loss of much valuable theory and background, which means that the new generation of teachers is increasingly out of step with the development of teachers in the rest of Europe. There is also a strong case to be made for suggesting that the real 'partnerships' that we should be developing extend beyond the boundaries of the UK alone and that all beginning teachers should receive some of their experience in a country other than their own, in Europe or elsewhere.

The current shift in terminology from 'education' to 'training' is not simply semantic; it is symptomatic of a government policy which is deeply suspicious of 'theory', expertise and what it perceives as the 'educational establishment', of which teacher educators are perceived to be a large and sinister component. Such policies are unlikely to be reversed and they have their echoes across the Atlantic with the development of professional training schools and the work of such pressure groups as 'the Holmes Group'.

Our experience of the changes suggests that when it is done well there can be much benefit from the new partnerships that are being developed. At the present time the nature of mentoring is much under discussion and there is a positive explosion in the publication of books on the mentoring process and on proposals for mentor training. It was this that led to our perception of the necessity for the present volune. Too many of the books so far published in this field, though often of great value, have tended towards generalizations about the role of the mentor. There is certainly a place for more in the way of subject specific books on mentoring. Clearly, except in the most general terms of classroom management, there is a real difference between the problems and needs of the beginning English teacher and those of a prospective science teacher. Even in management terms, running a science lab is clearly demanding in a different way from the demands of effectively managing a drama lesson. The experienced teacher will do all these things well, and often instinctively. Explaining *how to do them* to a beginning teacher calls for special qualities and skills; it is by no means always the case that the good teacher of school pupils is a good teacher of students.

The author of this book, Andrew Goodwyn, has a wide experience of the different models of mentoring that are being developed in association with different forms of partnerships with schools. He is by no means negative about the changes, but he is by no means uncritical of the changes either. The need for a clear account of the potential and hazards of the mentoring of beginning English teachers is undeniable; and this is what Andrew Goodwyn has sought to provide. The book is carefully grounded in a specific view of English teaching and is aware of the need to develop student teachers, newly qualified teachers and mentors alongside each other. It would serve as an ideal text to use for mentor training conferences and as a stimulus to local debates about the mentoring process.

My personal view is that, uncritically adopted, there are considerable potential dangers in the mentoring model. The first is the establishment of a *status quo* in the schools as the norm; we are, after all, preparing the teachers of tomorrow as well as those who will serve in the schools today. As I write this introduction my present generation of students are taking part in an intensive

workshop on desk top publishing and acquiring skills that will be of immediate use to them in their work in schools but which will also be an invaluable
resource for the schools of the future, a theme with which a forthcoming
volume in this series, *English for Tomorrow*, with which Andrew has also been
associated, will be concerned. We also have to find ways of avoiding too great
a dependence by students upon their mentors, leading to the uncritical adop-
tion of a particular teaching style. In a subject in which people are so personally
engaged as English, too, there will always be clashes of values and beliefs: the
problems that can arise because of clashes between mentor and student, the
differences between their perceptions of their roles, can lead to conflicts which
need to be resolved and which call for skill and experience by the more
'neutral' representative of the HEI. This may especially be the case when the
models of 'partnership' between schools and HEIs are based upon whole-
school partnerships rather than when these are established, usually much more
successfully, at a subject level.

What is needed is a model of the mentoring process that takes full account
of the interaction of mentor, student and HEI lecturer and which recognizes
the need to provide a context in which each member of the triad can learn
from each of the others. Andrew Goodwyn's timely contribution to this series
points us in this direction and recognizes the subtlety of the human relations
involved in mentoring in a way not always evidenced by some of the schemes
currently in action in schools.

Introduction

When prospective teachers of English, keen to secure a place on a PGCE course, come for interview and talk about why they are there, they almost invariably begin by talking, very enthusiastically, about how they have always loved to read. They can often remember the covers of individual books that still bring them a glow of pleasure, however many years later the occasion. For many such interviews I have the good fortune to be working in partnership with an experienced English teacher from a local school. After such an interview it is very common for that teacher to comment wryly on how little time such enthusiastic novices will have for reading once they become full-time teachers. Such a moment always reminds me of why the first assignment on the PGCE course for new student teachers is, to me, so important. The students are asked to investigate their own reading history, to reflect on reading in school and to begin to recognize how unusual they may perhaps have been as a child reader and how very much more unusual they have become as an adult who devotes much time to reading.

In its particular way, this typical moment highlights the essence of this book. In the interview we seem to have the enthusiastic and properly naive student teacher, the experienced and overworked, perhaps slightly cynical, teacher and the university lecturer, preoccupied with ideas and 'theory'. In fact we have nothing so simplistic. The 'naive' student teacher can be aged anything from 22 to 55 and comes with a head full of quite concrete ideas about the best way to teach English. The conscientious and dedicated teacher in question will very likely be looking after that, or a very similar, student teacher for five months the following year and helping that individual to begin to become a skilful and reflective teacher of English. I, as the university lecturer, at least attempt to be the facilitator and supporter of that future partnership, and that role requires, among other things, a great deal of practical and logistical management. We each have a part to play and job to do, with distinct but highly complementary roles. What is most certain is that the role of that English teacher as a mentor has become properly far more important but equally far more challenging.

In fact, the increasing emphasis on school-based initial teacher education has placed vastly increased responsibility on English teachers in schools. An increasing number of teachers have become the mentors of student teachers in school and, often, also of newly qualified teachers. The mentor role is usually undertaken in partnership with teacher education departments in universities and colleges. A number of models of mentorship are developing around the country; some are in line with best practice and some are profoundly unsatisfactory. Simultaneously, schools are suffering severe budget cuts, the Teacher Training Agency is reviewing all in-service provision, enrolments on higher degree courses are generally down and the advisory service is dwindling across the country.

Given this difficult and changing context, it seems pertinent to provide a book for English teachers that examines the role of the mentor in the school, specifically within the complex and notoriously personal domain of English teaching. This book needs to make the mentor role the central focus, but to examine it within a wider view of the continuing, as well as initial, development of teachers. It tries both to be eminently practical, with plenty of direct suggestions of how to manage this developing role, and to provide an understanding of the concept of reflective practice. It examines critically the nature of mentorship and questions some of the simplistic arguments put forward in support of school-based 'training'. Overall, it attempts to help the mentors of student, newly qualified and experienced English teachers to feel confident and clear about what they can achieve in this crucial role. It also places mentorship at the centre of a process for improving the profession of English teaching in the long term.

Chapter 1 explores the development of student teachers of English during their training year. It provides some overview of the way the PGCE has changed nationally and defines the nature of the year from the students' perspective – looking at how some courses are organized as examples and considering the concept of 'partnership' in detail in relation to one well developed course. It discusses some general issues about student teacher development and offers a historical dimension considering some of the losses as well as the gains of more school-based teacher education. It attempts to provide a clear picture of the context in which mentors are working.

Chapter 2 provides an examination of some aspects of English subject teaching, looking at how it is viewed by others, and especially by student teachers who are preparing to join the profession. This chapter provides readers with an understanding of the personal models that student teachers generally, and future English teachers in particular, bring with them to their training year. Generally it will help teachers to appreciate the nature of the student teacher's perspective and it is illustrated with quotations from student teachers and with some cases exemplifying how their ideas often interfere with their initial experiences. It introduces the idea of the reflective practitioner as a long-term aim for all English teachers.

Chapter 3 concentrates on the role of the mentor as the manager of student teachers' learning. It sets out what we know about the phases of learning to teach and illustrates ways of helping student teachers through these phases. It draws extensively on research into the mentor role generally and my own research over the years, and uses examples and quotations from mentors and student teachers themselves. It puts forward a model of the mentor as going beyond working with student teachers and extends the idea of the reflective practitioner. It also examines the tensions inherent in the mentor's role and how, in certain situations and without adequate resources, the role becomes untenable. The chapter should be especially helpful for mentors in preparing for the role and reviewing its development.

Chapter 4 places great stress on the human element in mentoring and examines the need for mentors to be student-centred in their definition of the role. It provides a framework, drawn from counselling, for working closely with student teachers experiencing the stresses and triumphs of learning to teach. The chapter should help mentors to draw on their existing range of skills as teachers to provide motivation and support for student teachers, while managing to move them forward throughout their time in school. The emphasis throughout is on the mentor as a professional, sensitive figure who can help student teachers to solve some problems and to face up to others that are going to require many years of teaching experience and reflection. It concludes by considering the mentor's own needs and sense of self-esteem.

Chapter 5 begins by examining the crucial issue of assessment and the mentor's vital role in the process. It provides scope for analysis of the competence model and helps mentors to see the demands of this type of assessment of student teachers. Using this idea of assessing development as a starting point, it then considers the first two years of English and the role of the mentor and of the department and school during this period, introducing the idea of the departmental mentor. It includes sections on appraisal, Ofsted inspections and in-service training, and places the mentor in a key role in terms of helping new English teachers to settle into the profession.

Chapter 6 concludes the book with a review of the long-term development of English teachers into genuinely independent reflective practitioners. It provides a more in-depth and critical look at the concept of the reflective practitioner and it examines the idea of the highly accomplished teacher, both in itself and as a role model. It outlines how good departments foster and support the long-term development of teachers and how the role of mentor can assist this development for some teachers. It offers some ideas about the ways in which departments and teachers can continue the process of development even when they are fully experienced. It considers how the move to school-based initial teacher education will need long-term monitoring and support if it is to become established as a high-quality development.

I have tried to write the book in as readable and as direct a way as possible and to allow myself the occasional aside. I have tried to keep the text uncluttered, but wherever I think readers need the evidence or the references in the text I have supplied them. However, I have also used just a few endnotes for readers who want more information or want to look for further evidence or suggestions for reading. As so many members of the English teaching profession are female, I have adopted the use of 'she' throughout. I hope the book is of some use to the English teaching profession, and particularly to those who take on the extra demand of helping not only children but their colleagues as well.

1 The potential of partnership: mentors and school-based initial teacher education

Considering that teaching as a profession is often seen, certainly by the general public, as a worthy, but rather dull, vocation, it is perhaps surprising that teacher education itself should be such a controversial area. Every developed society declares that it needs teachers and, apparently, highly values every one of them, usually employing many hundreds of thousands, relying on them, if for no other reason than for keeping children busy for most of the working day. However, teacher education certainly has become controversial and, at the time of writing, has just undergone a very major set of changes that may well continue over the coming years. I shall return to the historical dimension later in the chapter.

The most immediate result of these changes has been to make the lives of many teachers both more challenging and, potentially, more fulfilling. Many teachers are now charged with the responsibility of 'teaching' student teachers as well as children. I stress 'teaching' them because readers of this book will know what a highly complex and problematic term 'teaching' actually is; they will not reduce it to some simplistic notion like 'delivering the National Curriculum' as if it came in a wheelbarrow. Teachers know that there is a great deal more to teaching than another term, such as 'instruction', would imply. Equally, there is far more to inducting people into the teaching profession than just telling them, or simply showing them, 'what to do'.

This chapter sets out to help those teachers to put the task of becoming excellent mentors, as well as excellent classroom teachers, into some perspective. The chapter is the most general in the book and draws least extensively on specific English-related matters. However, most schools that have taken on any aspect of teacher education now find themselves supporting a significant number of student teachers. Any English teacher may well have to work with student teachers from quite different disciplines, as well as those that share her lifelong preference for English.

Mentors' own teacher education

Most teachers currently working in schools underwent some kind of 'teacher training course' themselves and, in my personal experience, the great majority, and that includes myself, look back with mixed feelings on that experience. A common view is that those courses paid far too much attention to 'theory' and nothing like enough attention to the demands of the actual classroom. As each reader is now probably reflecting on her own course, and before I provide a brief overview of changes to teacher education, it is worth commenting directly on these memories and their current value to a teacher who is considering what is involved in being a good mentor.

Many teachers recall their teaching practice as a very difficult and stressful time for which they felt under-prepared. Any reader will appreciate that such views are often based on dim and now distant memories, but I would also emphasize that for any potential mentor these memories might repay close attention. Whatever process we devise to induct people into teaching, it is likely to be stressful for the participants and, as I shall discuss later, a degree of such challenge is not only inevitable but actually desirable. However, too much stress causes pain and possibly damage, making it difficult for people to function in any meaningful way. A genuine problem for experienced teachers is that they really do find it hard, at times, to recall the difficulties of early teaching experiences. They are now so capable and competent that it is quite difficult to understand why a struggling student 'just will not take in my advice!' So, as we review the changes to teacher education courses it is highly productive for any reader to reflect on and to recall her early experiences in a systematic way, and to review those now, rather as a novelist might do, as material, as a useful resource to learn something new from and to help with a new or extended role.

This self-examination is important as a process rather than as an 'exercise'; telling a student teacher about how challenging teaching was once, for this now competent professional, helps both the student and the mentor to establish common ground and to develop an empathetic relationship. Obviously, for each new student teacher, the mentor needs to repeat that process and, in so doing, is likely to become more adept and more skilful at drawing out parallels and learning points for each individual, and inevitably different, student teacher.

Another vital element in such systematic reflection relates to the mentor's role in designing and working on a teacher education course. Mentors are now, quite rightly, part of a course team that, in collaboration, plans, operates and reviews every teacher education course, and this will be further discussed.

As an obvious starting point, a mentor really does need to have an overview of how her particular course works in considerable detail. Each course has a period of development and a history; this history articulates with the national picture, especially now that teacher education is effectively a national and highly controlled system. As mentors review the courses that inducted them into the profession, perhaps in conversation with other mentors, they will be more able to analyse and reflect upon the design and quality of the current school-based models. Some sense of the more general history of teacher education can only enhance this capability. When a mentor reflects, consciously and systematically, on her own experiences as a student teacher, there is a good chance that a great deal of useful knowledge will emerge.

The national context

Readers might like to begin by guessing the date of this comment about how the government should reform teacher training.

> The part of the field which we are to examine has long been a battleground for the expert, and many questions call for discussion. What, for example, should be the purpose of professional training? – its character and duration? Where should it be given, and by whom? . . . At what age should it commence? – and is a system of apprenticeship desirable?
>
> (Quoted in Gardner, 1993: 21)

This contemporary sounding comment was published in 1923 and it might surprise some readers, as teacher education is constantly criticized for being 'modern' and 'trendy',[1] that its beginnings occur in the early nineteenth century (Bernbaum et al., 1985; Fish, 1989; Gardner, 1993). It was originally a monitorial system, based in schools, with no involvement with any outside agencies. In 1846 the Kay–Shuttleworth, pupil–teacher approach was adopted, which mainly emphasized practical skills but also provided some time for moral and spiritual education. The 1870 Education Act introduced the first real compulsory, universal education, and this immediately put pressure on the government, not only for more teachers, but for more specialized teachers. Over the next 50 years this pressure steadily pushed the training of teachers into teacher preparation colleges, where student teachers underwent an academic course and a vocational preparation. It is striking that Herbert Ward, the Board of Education's Chief Inspector for the training of teachers in the 1920s, wrote in 1928:

> teachers should be trained to do their work, not following blind tradition, or even immersed in the particulars of technique, but with some knowledge of the philosophical bases of teaching and of education . . . and if students do not get it during their year of training it is hard to come by in later years. We will try to be as practical as we can, and we are sincerely anxious to give our students adequate

experience in actual teaching. But we cannot be satisfied to remain on the level of technique.

(Gardner, 1993: 31)

This comment may help to reassure readers that the pendulum on teacher education has swung from school to college and is now, almost certainly, swinging back towards school. History is showing us that pendulums will swing and that they rarely come to a point of total rest.

The system between the wars was relatively stable but 1944 brought the introduction of universal secondary education and, as more demands were placed on teachers, so the teacher training colleges were expected to provide longer and even more specialized courses. During this period, and on into the 1970s, education was struggling to establish itself as an academic discipline to rank alongside other traditional disciplines, and teaching was attempting to become a profession with some comparability to the law and medicine. This combination inevitably emphasized the academic elements in what was expected to become an all-graduate profession.

This was also a period of great change, development and reform in education generally. The comprehensive movement was becoming firmly established, bringing together teachers from the very divided grammar and secondary modern traditions. It is also worth noting that this was a time when English in education became a real field of research. In 1970, James Britton produced *Language and Learning*, a book which had a huge impact on English. John Dixon's *Growth through English* (Dixon, 1966) helped to define the whole personal growth model of English that has been the foundation for much English teaching ever since (see Chapter 2). By 1975, the Bullock Report (HMSO, 1975) sparked the Language Across the Curriculum movement, which affected every secondary school in the UK. It was the era of the Schools Council, a body that constantly initiated research into education and sponsored experiment and school-based curriculum change.

These decades of great innovation and dynamism continue to resonate with our work today. However, this explosion of ideas and research findings attracted attention in many negative ways. The late 1960s and early 1970s are also the time of the Black Papers, when Brian Cox, later self-styled champion of English teachers (Cox, 1991, 1992) was lambasting every English teacher in the country, claiming that 'Anarchy is becoming fashionable . . . there is great danger that the traditional high standards of English education are being overthrown . . . the grammar school concepts of discipline and work are treated with contempt' (quoted in Cox, 1992: 145). The Bullock Report was, ironically, an accidental product of the then Education Secretary's (Margaret Thatcher's) attempt to instigate a review of the supposedly falling reading standards.

Despite this reactionary backlash, the role of teachers in education and the status of educational theory were really powerful at that time and they were setting much of the agenda for the whole country. The majority of people generating these theories were people in teacher education; in the case of English, figures such as James Britton, Douglas Barnes and Harold Rosen. The theories[2] they generated challenged many traditions, not only about teaching but also about what schooling was for, its very purpose (Goodson and Medway, 1990). Much of such theory challenged social ideas of privilege and traditional elitism, as did the principles of comprehensive education. In secondary English this period marks the transition from a hundred years of domination by concepts of the literary, to which Leavis had given such immense energy in the 1930s, to a new era preoccupied with language and identity.

It is important to recognize, then, that it is not just 'teacher education' that has been recently and seriously threatened, it is also the whole idea that teachers can play a distinctive part in improving society by changing children. The rapid developments in English, which found their practical expression in coursework and oral work, have also been constantly attacked since their inception, and are a part of the same reform movement as that inspired by teacher educators of the 1960s and 1970s. Most of the recent changes to English and to teacher education, whatever the rhetoric in which they have been wrapped up, have been driven by the desire to deprofessionalize and deskill teachers, to remove as much of the academic status of education as possible in order, eventually, to reduce the scope and status of teachers themselves. From the mid-1980s onwards there has been increasing pressure on teacher education, mainly from government, to become 'more relevant'. No one quarrels with the *idea* of relevance but its interpretation has been highly problematic.

In the college and polytechnic sector, during the 1970s and 1980s, the Council for National Academic Awards (CNAA) became increasingly powerful and stringent in its regulations. There is evidence that the CNAA was, in fact, an early agent in creating school–college partnerships and that in the non-university sector there were some useful experiments in involving teachers far more meaningfully in teacher education. However, the university sector that generally managed PGCE routes was left independent until the emergence of CATE in 1983.

The Council for the Accreditation of Teacher Education (CATE) emerged as the result of an increasingly determined attempt to 'shake up' university education departments. In 1981, the HMI produced a discussion paper, 'Teacher training in the secondary school: the implications of the HMI survey' (January). This document argued for far more school/higher education links and criticized courses for being theory dominated. In 1983, 'Teaching in schools: the content of initial training' put forward far more strident views about the need for imparting basic skills to student teachers, and again criticized courses for being too removed from practice. Later that year, the government White Paper, *Teaching Quality*, announced the creation of a committee to oversee, at local and national level, the training of teachers. It brought in the notion that all teacher education tutors should have 'recent and relevant' experience. This is another idea with considerable merit; almost all secondary-focused teacher educators have many years' experience in classrooms and as heads of subject departments, but their experience may become relatively distant. Typically, no resources were allocated to fund this idea, and it also ignored the fundamental point that being a teacher educator is very different from teaching in school. It is a full-time job in which experience plays a very considerable part. The most positive way to look at this is that in some of the 'new' school-based courses, HEI (higher education institution) tutors are spending a great deal of time in schools. Some of this time is devoted to working with students, some with staff and some to research; there is more than one way to have relevant experience.

Over the next few years of the 1980s, CATE increasingly prescribed what education departments had to do to be accredited, and it placed further impositions on lecturers in education. Whether they were good ideas or not, they were not the result of any consultation, and the HMI became more and more involved in 'visiting', with a clear agenda for getting at the 'educational establishment'. In 1984, DES Circular 3/84 set out a series of criteria on the basis of which courses would be accredited.

The period from 1988 onwards has seen these concerted forces turning their critique into legislation. Part of this effort has been directed at circumventing teacher education entirely. For example, the licensed teachers scheme, launched in 1988, placed people immediately in schools to learn 'on the job'. The employer had discretion about the extent of initial training, if any, that the licensed teacher should receive. This scheme has had little real impact on the profession, but it did place, perhaps accidentally, a useful stress on the concept of mentorship. Its concept was a very limited one and may have discredited that role in some places, but it did at least recognize that, for there to be more systematic learning about teaching in school, there would be a need for new and rather different roles for classroom teachers.

In 1989, the articled teacher scheme was launched. This was a two-year postgraduate course, in which students would spend 80 per cent of their time in schools. It was taken up by a number of consortia, consisting of local authorities and higher education institutions, and has had a small impact on overall numbers.

Probably the most significant change was the entry of the Open University into teacher education. The Open University was given a £2.4 million grant, in 1992, to establish its place in the new teacher education 'market place'. From a base of 1300 students it had expanded to provide 12,000 places per year in 1995–6. This has had a useful and positive effect, enabling many potential teachers living in remote areas to find a way into qualifying as teachers. However, it also means, very frequently in practice, that Open University students who find themselves in schools with a strong link with a HEI actually get the benefits of those links through coincidence and not planning. This is not a criticism of the Open University's distance learning model, but it is a comment on the inequities of a system under pressure and with considerable signs of fragmentation and eventual chaos.

By this stage, 1993, matters were moving very rapidly. Circular 9/92 (DFE, 1992) announced, in great detail, the exact criteria for what would be the new generation of secondary, teacher education courses. Circular 14/93 (DFE, 1993a) has introduced the same for primary courses. The new requirements came into effect for secondary courses in September 1994. The main principle of these changes is that schools should become the centres of teacher education and the leading partners in the design and operation of courses; implicitly, rather than directly, this also made clear that classroom teachers would be expected to take the major role in inducting student teachers into the profession. In 1993 there was another and very definitive White Paper, *The Government's Proposals for the Reform of Initial Teacher Training* (DFE, 1993b), which led to the 1994 Education Act. This Act abolished CATE and set up the Teacher Training Agency (TTA), with considerable powers (but no accountability) to control the initial teacher education and, eventually, professional development of every teacher in the country. As with all such centralizing, control mechanisms, the TTA has been given absolute control over the funding of all teacher education courses. English teachers tend to get rather tired of being the guardians of the language and having to know everything about words, but I suspect that readers of this book will find the very title 'Teacher Training Agency' offensive in its reductive and narrow implications about a vocation that is so sophisticated and complex. One, so far minor, effect of these changes has been to provide consortia of schools with the opportunity to devise and run their own PGCE courses in their entirety. Only a few consortia have so far emerged and they make use of local HEIs for some of the course design and for some teaching.

For a mentor it is vital to have a sketch of these changes. It is worth considering first how an entirely school-based model of teacher education last existed in the nineteenth century. There was nothing *wrong* with that idea in the context of the nineteenth century, it is simply not the same context as the twentieth; for example, we now have universal compulsory education until the age of sixteen, whereas universal schooling barely existed in the early nineteenth century. No amount of nostalgia will change facts like that, and that century's ideas do not look like offering a model for the twenty-first. Second, it is obvious to anyone working in school that, whatever it was like 150 years ago, the job of a teacher now is incredibly demanding and complicated, and continues to be more so; again, one only has to consider the development of media and information technologies to recognize what a huge difference they make on children and their learning.

The key point here is that these changes in teacher education have not been orchestrated to help teachers in schools, who were not, as it happens, asked whether they wished teacher education to develop this way. These changes have been dominated by a relentless attempt to disconnect higher education from teacher education and to develop forms of teacher 'training' that are, simply, cheap. Most teachers that I have worked with have been horrified by these aims and they reject them for the philistine attack that they truly are. In some ways the nature of the movement that has coordinated these changes can be seen more clearly in some of the journalistic pieces of the late 1980s and early 1990s, where politicians like Rhodes Boyson castigate teacher education as the root of all evil (see Protherough and Atkinson, 1991: Chapter 4).

However, despite the unhappy genesis of these changes, I am certainly an advocate of the best kind of school-based teacher education and consider that many of these dangerous and politically motivated changes have nevertheless produced some valuable steps forward for the partners now committed to initial teacher education. I feel it best to put to one side the way in which these changes have been imposed on the teaching profession and to examine them, critically, as they are and as we might use them as the basis for teacher education into the twenty-first century.

School-based teacher education: the current model

A mentor can be much more informed by having some overview of what the national requirements are for teacher education courses, and through such an understanding can gain a much more powerful insight into why the particular course within which she operates is constructed in its present form. It is also increasingly the case, at least in my experience, that, in total, fewer schools are now involved directly in teacher education, but those schools are much more heavily involved than they used to be. One inevitable and very positive result for those schools, and their student teachers, is that they are organizing themselves to assimilate and support student teachers throughout the year. Having student teachers 'around' has become a norm for some schools and, even more particularly, for some departments. One side-effect of this change has been to attract even more student teachers to those schools. It is quite possible then that a school may have a major partnership with one HEI, several students from another, similar institution, a licensed teacher and the occasional Open University student.

Inevitably, such 'growth', may be problematic. One reason for it, in an era of local financial management, may well be senior management's wish to capitalize on their 'investment' in teacher education. To put it crudely, the more student teachers, the more the 'income'. It is difficult for a school to judge the appropriate 'load' and to place a financial value on the other kinds of support offered by the partnership HEIs. For a mentor the issue may come down to how much identifiable time is allocated to being a mentor. I am stressing then that the overall organization of these courses might seem complicated, even remote, but the effect of that organization is in a direct relationship to some aspects of the potential quality of mentoring.

The school's openness to school-based teacher education will not usually include all members of staff; some may be actively opposed to it. Some of those staff who reject the new model may be in a department where the majority of staff are keen to build a partnership; such tensions can cause considerable frictions and make a mentor's job very awkward. However, those positive members of the department may well be able to convince sceptical colleagues by demonstrating how the new model actually works. Yet as the whole school becomes more teacher education oriented, less involved staff may become increasingly disaffected and 'anti-student'. Every work environment has its stresses and strains, and I must have heard now, many times, that 'you can't get a cup of coffee round here any more with all these students in the queue before you'. Such off-hand remarks are symptomatic of stress and irritation and, in that sense, must be taken seriously; such remarks hurt people's feelings out of all proportion to the speaker's intention. School-based teacher education puts a strain on staff whether they wish to be involved in the actual process or not.

What I am emphasizing is that school-based teacher education does affect the very fabric of a school's life. It always did to some extent, but now the effect is constant and powerful. A mentor has many reasons, then, for having a clear picture of exactly how a course operates and also why it differs from other courses. To help mentors to gain a clear picture of the context in which they are expected to make a vital contribution, I summarize below the requirements of Circular 9/92 (DFE, 1992).

- All secondary and middle schools, sixth form colleges and tertiary colleges in England and Wales, both maintained and independent, should have the opportunity to become partners in teacher training if they wish to do so.
- Schools have the initiative and should approach HEIs to find out what they offer (in practice I am not aware that this happens; not surprisingly, schools are usually approached by their prospective higher education partners).
- The HEI has to make clear its criteria for the formation of partnerships, including the use of indicators as evidence of quality of teaching and learning.
- Schools have to describe the contributions they can make to student teachers' training and to the planning and management of courses; this includes describing their own approach to, and record in, providing professional development for their own staff, general school facilities, the educational position of children with special needs and opportunities for extra-curricular activities.
- Schools have to specify the subjects they are prepared to offer and the number of students they are prepared to take.
- HEIs can reject a school's offer but they have to make explicit their reasons for rejection (schools, however, can pick and choose HEIs as they like, offering no criteria).
- The HEI can subsequently have its accreditation withdrawn if a school is shown to have been treated arbitrarily or unreasonably.

- The overall emphasis is said to be on the joint responsibility for the planning and management of courses and the selection, training and assessment of students, but the balance of responsibilities will vary.
- Schools have the leading responsibility for training students to teach specialist subjects, to assess pupils and to manage classes, for supervising students and for assessing their competence in these respects.
- There is a set of national competencies against which all student teachers must be assessed.
- HEIs have to ensure the academic validation of courses, present them for accreditation and present the actual awards.
- HEIs also have to ensure that the national requirement for all student teachers to have significant experience *of at least two schools* is carried out – this means negotiating two placements for each student. (This requirement partly explains why some courses look very different as schools and HEIs have negotiated different patterns for these placements.)
- Student teachers must spend two-thirds of their course in school – on current PGCE courses this means 24 weeks out of 36 in schools – and they must have 'substantial experience in at least two schools'.

These are the basic requirements which all partnerships must both observe and interpret to create workable courses. There is room for difference of emphasis and interpretation between courses but the framework is not changeable under current legislation. Each partnership has to agree the length and scope of placements, the actual responsibilities of each individual HEI tutor and teacher involved and how the various assessments will be carried out and recorded. Each partnership also needs groups who can meet regularly to do the joint planning and management and who evaluate and review the course, year by year. As schools do not have to commit themselves for more than one year, whereas the HEI is permanently committed, such groups will be likely to change in personnel and will need ways of identifying and supporting schools, and teachers, at different stages of expertise in relation to student teachers. For example, a school may wish to join a partnership scheme which has had no experience of student teachers for many years. A school may start in a partnership and then drop out for a period and then wish to come back. A school may be consistently in the partnership but constantly rotate its departmental involvement. Managing the course is not, then, some static rubber stamp activity; it is demanding and time-consuming, and needs the dynamic involvement of all concerned, particularly of those people who work most closely and intensely with the students, their subject mentors.

Course structures: an example

As course structures properly differ between partnerships, there would be little point in listing, comparing and contrasting endless, minor differences.

However, I am going, briefly, to describe the course that I know best, to provide any reader with a concrete example and also to acknowledge that my close involvement with such a course will undoubtedly have influenced my thinking and may help to explain the nature of my particular 'vision'. I should also make it clear from the start that I am an advocate for this course, but not a merely partial one. Extensive contacts with colleagues in other parts of the country and some other countries, as well as work as an external examiner in several HEIs, has provided me with what I feel is a reasonable basis for putting this course forward, not as the model, but certainly as a good model. I think that providing a reader with a very real example should offer something concrete and exact to use in 'weighing up' other courses.

Fortunately for the participants, this model was already being developed before the flurry of dictats in the early 1990s. It began its life a year before the 1994 deadline and had been three years in development before its introduction; at the time of writing it is in its third year and has been through some useful and properly negotiated fine tuning throughout that time. At all stages its shape and form have been negotiated but, inevitably and in my view, quite properly, its main impetus has in fact come from HEI tutors. This impetus does not downgrade the contribution of school-based colleagues, it simply recognizes that HEIs feel responsible for such planning and course design and have a vast deal of experience to draw upon. The course team, in this case, had long felt a need to increase the time spent by students in school, but only on the basis of increasing the quality of that experience. It is notable that schools resisted, for a long time, the idea of students spending more weeks in school; they were, very properly, sceptical about what students would gain, especially when their own job was educating children at what was, because of the ceaseless demands of the shifting sands of the National Curriculum, a very difficult time. However, the introduction of the national framework left us all with the question of how to make the most of the 'new' time in school.

For a mentor, working in a school-based course, it is important to view the whole process by which students arrive in her particular school, and this, inevitably, begins many months before the year of the course. Long before student teachers arrive in the September of their actual course, they first have to be interviewed and selected. During the months of October, November and December there will be a flood of applications for a relatively popular course like English. Mentors are jointly responsible for this process and are invited to help with selection and then to be present at interview as often as possible. On the course in question, interviews for English are arranged to fit in with the timetables of those mentors who have volunteered to play a role in the process. Candidates are asked to visit a comprehensive school for at least a whole day near to the interview and to come prepared to talk about this experience. Current practice is to invite them in groups of three, to provide a half an hour briefing about the course, jointly presented by the tutor and the mentor, and then to see each candidate for about half an hour, dividing question time between tutor and mentor. Even at that stage there needs to be a careful discussion with each candidate about transport and domestic arrangements, as the complexities of placing all students in two schools are logistically enormous. If a student is offered a place then she is provided with plenty of suggestions for reading and a range of strategies to prepare herself, including, for example, the exhortation to devote time to developing some computer competence. Finally, students are asked to prepare, and send as soon as possible, a position statement, putting forward what they feel they bring to English teaching and defining some of the goals they want to achieve before the course begins, commenting on some of the aims they have in becoming effective teachers of English. This position statement is revised throughout the PGCE year and each student must complete a 'final' version at the end of the course as part of her preparation for initial professional development.

The course operates, as decreed, with 12 weeks at university and 24 weeks in two schools, a total of 5 weeks in school A and 19 weeks in school B; there are also three days in primary school taken from within the 24-week period. At this point it is worth stressing that some mentors may find themselves working with more than one structure at once and that they may wish to influence their school's policy on teacher education by expressing their preferences for one model over another. A key point may well be how closely the mentor gets to know each student teacher. For example, the more a student divides her time between two schools, the less time there is to form a close relationship with one school and, therefore, one mentor.

The chronology of the course in focus can be summed up as an initial period of two weeks' orientation at university, two weeks' intensive observation in school A and then two weeks back at university reflecting on school A and preparing for school B. This is now mid-October and students undertake a long, second phase, two consecutive days per week at university, followed by three days in school, in local jargon the '2 + 3' (I am sure every course has evolved its local terminological nuances). From mid-February the students spend all their time in school B, undertaking what most people would call the block practice; on this course the practice is roughly divided in half, depending on Easter itself, by the spring holidays. At the end of this period students have a further two-week university block. They then return to school A to undertake a negotiated project or, in a few cases, to undertake more teaching in order to reach a competent level to pass the course. That leaves one concluding week at university.

The course has two main strands, method studies and complementary studies, given roughly equal time at university. Method studies are the student teachers' chosen specialisms; complementary studies tries to cover the host of other issues that student teachers need to know about, from health and safety in school to working with children with special needs. I will not overburden the reader with detail here but just pick out two essential factors that, in my view, make the course a genuine partnership: first, the interconnection between complementary studies and school-based studies; second, English work in both locations.

The majority of schools take eight students in four subject pairs, although there are many variations to accommodate individual schools; small schools, for example, take about four students. In each school there is a professional tutor (this has become a fairly standard national term) responsible for all student teachers throughout the course, for providing the students with experience of the pastoral system and for coordinating the complementary studies programme in the school. All professional tutors meet together once a year to review course matters.

Each individual professional tutor is given a half a day per week to meet the students and to run a school-based seminar. These seminars focus on key whole school issues. For example, in the 2 + 3 phase, the students might have an overview lecture about special needs, followed, after a break, by the meeting of their seminar group. This group will be made up, normally, of eight students from one school and eight from another. (These two schools are twinned and at each phase when students change school they move from one of the twinned schools to the other.) In this way the group always has a real, known context to refer to. The university's complementary studies tutor (CST) is the link tutor with both schools, and visits each school every other week, attending the school-based seminar. That particular week, the focus in school will be special needs, so that the students can learn how national policies and recent research are interpreted in school. A student teacher may eventually select special needs as the subject for her whole school study. As well as seeing students at individual tutorials spaced throughout the year, the CST visits each student once during the block practice. In this course model there is a heavy commitment of time by all involved staff, but especially by HEI staff who travel to school every week for most of the year.

The university-based English programme is jointly planned with the mentors of English students in school. These mentors are given the title of supervising teacher of English (ST), and they meet method tutors (MT) twice a year for a full day's discussion. These meetings are very highly valued by everyone involved and have been an excellent forum for course and professional development. At one such meeting the English programme is reviewed, and agreed, so that each mentor knows what is happening at the university in any given week. This allows for a mentor to help the student teacher to see connections between university and school work. This connection might be at a relatively simple level early on in the course; for example, if the university session examines the teaching of poetry, then the mentor might simply look for any lessons that week where poetry is featured, so that the student can see poetry teaching in action. Later in the course, as the student becomes more able to take in detail through observation, a mentor might follow up a second university session on poetry by also directing the student's attention to what kind of teaching is happening. Can the student see evidence of a reader response

approach being adopted and, if so, how successfully? (see Chapter 2 for further illustration of this point.) Other strong links include inviting some STs in
to run university sessions, and others are involved in interviewing and selecting future student teachers of English. Over the year each ST has a period per
week per student to meet the students and to discuss progress; this is an absolutely key element in the whole programme.

During the students' time in school they will be visited twice by an MT
before the block practice, once just before and once just after Christmas, and
then at least four times during the block for observations of teaching. This
number of visits (which is far higher than for most current PGCE courses)
ensures that the tutor knows the department, as well as the individual mentor,
and can develop a good understanding of the context in which each student
teacher is learning to teach. Towards the end of the block an external examiner for English will visit about a quarter of the students to check that assessment is accurate and fair by university and school staff. This constant flow of
information and personnel between the institutions makes the English part of
the programme very visible to all parties. As English tutors are usually CSTs
as well, but deliberately in different schools so that the two functions are not
blurred, this also ensures that both student teachers and mentors can speak to
people who know the whole course and who know how the two strands are
interwoven.

In this course model, student teachers are inducted very gradually into
teaching, moving from observation to small-scale participation to whole-class
teaching, and this approach will be discussed later in more depth (see Chapter
3). However, it is worth stressing at this point how powerful a role the mentor
can play by having a full picture of the student's programme and course
structure. There are constant opportunities to help the student teacher to
make connections between school-based and university-based work and reflect
on those connections in depth. There is no doubt that this places a very
considerable and constant responsibility on a mentor, which needs recognition
(and resources) from somewhere in the system.

The whole course is managed by a steering group made up of representatives from partnership schools and the university. This group is informed by
a host of other groups, such as:

- a staff–student consultative committee at which all students are given a
  voice, via seminar group representatives;
- groups that represent various schools in their combinations of twos and
  threes and their respective link tutors – these groups usually meet each year
  to review in-school arrangements and to plan for the subsequent year;
- regular meetings of subject mentors with university subject staff;
- a university PGCE staff group that meets at the beginning of each term to
  coordinate the programme and review finances, student placements and a
  host of other matters;

- a monitoring and evaluation group that constantly provides data and real feedback on the course to ensure that changes are the result of consultation and solid information;
- the university board for teacher education, which reviews the university's long-term role in teacher education at all levels;
- internal and external assessment meetings, for some of which external examiners are present to offer advice and to ensure fair treatment of students across the course.

There are numerous other meetings and endless, more informal exchanges, and this should give mentors some perspective on the scale of consultation and organization involved in running partnership schemes. Many schools also run their own internal meetings, bringing, for example, all subject mentors together.

In giving this brief summary of one course, I am aware of how much I have left out and of how much detail would be needed to paint the full colour picture of this one canvas. At some later points in the text I shall draw on this course for further examples of how mentors can play increasingly important roles in student development, but I hope that the overall point is very clear: mentors are full and active partners in the new partnerships and need an overview to make responsible and effective use of that role. Time is provided, in this course example, for joint course planning and evaluation with HEI tutors and, each week, for meetings with student teachers.

The student teacher's perspective

In Chapter 2, I shall discuss the way in which being a student teacher of English affects a student teacher's perceptions and attitudes to becoming a teacher. In this section I wish to look, relatively briefly, at two points about learning to become a teacher in the general sense, especially at the concepts and concerns that tend to fill up the horizons of some student teachers. Each point provides a starting point for a mentor who wishes to reflect on these broad concerns and to feel prepared to deal with the kinds of demands that student teachers make.

One major concern is the concept of a *vocation*. Teaching is described frequently, perhaps *ad nauseam*, as a vocation. Initially this sounds fine; student teachers have usually chosen teaching because they view it as a worthwhile and valuable job, not as well paid as some other jobs but worth doing because of its intrinsic rewards. In general terms there is nothing wrong with such a principled attitude, especially as it is, in essence, a genuine foundation for a dedicated career and as teaching is not, relatively speaking, well paid. However, teaching, as readers will know, is not a sentimental occupation. Student teachers, bringing such high ideals, must inevitably fall, and fall hard. A good mentor must also have some counselling skills (see Chapter 4), and the last thing I am suggesting is that any student teacher's ideals should be ignored or trivialized. On the contrary, those ideals need sympathy and support. When a student teacher first complains in exasperation about an awful class that ruined her lesson 'when she had put hours of work into it', we know that she is suffering from rejection. For a very few student teachers this experience is actually enough to put them off for good. They never really recover from the shock of rejection. However, this also means that they never reach the stage of recognizing how satisfying and genuinely demanding teaching actually is. The majority overcome rejection and gain some perspective upon it, but they benefit enormously from sympathetic support. If a student is suffering from this full sense of rejection then there is no point in discussing the lesson and saying, 'Well if you had done this and then that, then all would have been well.' The student needs general and sensitive support. I am stressing that a mentor will need to recognize when a student will not be receptive to advice but extremely in need simply of reassurance, comfort in fact. This does not mean that mentors themselves have to be sentimental, but they do have to provide emotional support at times of distress. It is useful for a mentor to recognize that a student is not really complaining or merely feeling self-pity; it is the strength of her vocational ideal that is being tested, and this needs sensitive handling. This whole area will be dealt with in depth in Chapter 4.

The second point, closely linked to the vocational issue, is the notion of *professionalism*. As well as setting themselves up by having high ideals, student teachers also have high expectations *of teachers*. Once again, this is a positive and admirable attitude: they feel they are joining a group of dedicated professionals. My own experience, working with students across a range of subjects, is that English student teachers have some of the very highest sets of expectations (readers, be warned!). Student teachers often remark with genuine shock on the 'awful' atmosphere in staff rooms, the pettiness, the back biting and so on. I noted above the kinds of comments generated by extras in the coffee queue; student teachers are extra sensitive to off-hand comments and in-jokes that make them feel left out. Equally, they are likely to be very critical of teachers and 'the way they speak to children'. So students may seem both over-sensitive when it suits them and hyper-critical when they feel like it; such a combination is likely to try the patience of any mentor.

However, for the mentor, this apparent contradiction can be put usefully into perspective by discussing with a student what professionalism is *in practice*. A mentor is in a pastoral role. A student teacher will need some protection from the casual comments of other staff and the uncomfortable feeling that they 'do not belong'. Other teachers are not being unprofessional, they are being human. Equally, teachers themselves will need some help when students make ill-judged and superficial criticisms about their truly professional work with children. Much of this part of the pastoral role is about facilitating good relationships and a mentor is the key facilitator. For an example of this need, I well remember a school ringing the university to complain about a student who had been in for a few days just to undertake some observation. The deputy head was adamant that this student should not be allowed to take the PGCE course, as she had seriously upset several experienced staff. When I got to the bottom of the situation I discovered the problem. For personal reasons the student had requested to undertake her initial observation at the end of the school year and not at the beginning of the term in mid-September. The university documentation, with advice to students, was written with the beginning of the year in mind. It advised the student to find out things such as whether the teacher knew the class well as yet, and whether the children had produced any interesting work so far, and so on. The student teacher in question, who was in fact a mature person, had naively asked astonished teachers, who had worked for a whole year with a group, questions such as 'Have you ever taught this group before?', 'Have they ever produced any good work?' and so on. The reader will see clearly what an effect such a mistake would create. The school was much happier when the problem was understood; however, the student teacher in question was revealing a lack of sensitivity that was to cause further problems. The student teacher was striving to be professional, but the effect was to give the opposite impression; a mentor, in this instance, would have to become a mediator.

These two examples about teaching as a vocation and about professionalism serve only as a starting point for mentors to begin to reflect on that role. Each example points up the multi-faceted nature of mentorship and the need to be a mediator. Being a mediator is not easy, but it is made easier and certainly more effective from a secure knowledge base. Some of that knowledge comes from years of subject teaching and this will be the focus of Chapter 2. However, mentorship makes very new and different demands from the classroom role and this is the focus of Chapters 3 and 4. Part of that knowledge base comes from an understanding of teacher education in a broad, national and historical sense; some needs to be very specific, local and contextual. These have been the main subjects of Chapter 1. Before we move into the close analysis of the role it is important to review some general issues about school-based teacher education to ensure that readers feel that their knowledge base is a sound one.

School-based teacher education: losses and gains

I am, as I stated above, an advocate of properly planned and well resourced school-based teacher education, but I am not in support of the *motivation* for its introduction, nor do I feel at all complacent that some of the recent gains in the quality of courses will be preserved. Before we move on to look closely at the 'Englishness' of student teachers of English (Chapter 2) and the specific role of the mentor (Chapters 3 and 4), it is important to review the current picture and to examine its strengths and weaknesses.

The first and most important point is that 'mentor' may have become quite a familiar term over the past few years, mostly in the commercial world in fact,[3] but the complexity and responsibility of the job, especially in schools, is a relatively new phenomenon. It is not that all good teachers have never done anything like this – on the contrary, they have much experience to draw on – it is that the demand has shifted from small to great: being a *professional mentor* now is an essential job for those who take it on. We must guard against the fact that the useful experience mentioned above does not, by any means, equate to preparation for high-level mentorship; nor is it any guarantee, under greatly changed circumstances, that the previous experience is of direct use in the present.

This change of the concept of mentorship typifies others, having a great potential for good, but simultaneously highlighting some concerns. In my view it gives proper status and an effective title to a key role in schools. It identifies for others the importance of that role and places it within a career and personal development context (see Chapters 5 and 6). However, it also identifies that resources and training are needed for the role to be effectively fulfilled. It also means that someone has to be found to undertake such a role, in a manner which ensures that a student teacher receives professional support of an equally high standard to that of all other schools in a partnership scheme. Not all mentors are approached thoughtfully. As one mentor commented, 'I had virtually no choice about participating in the scheme. I was asked in passing, in the corridor by a deputy, and several months later it was a fait accompli.' What should an HEI tutor do if she feels that a student teacher is not receiving such support, if the mentor turns out to be a poor one? It is schools that select their own mentors and, frequently, mentors are simply the persons who puts themselves forward to undertake the role; very occasionally the person who least resists the role ends up with mentorship thrust, uncomfortably, upon her. One mentor explained, 'There was some pressure put on the department by the head to accept students. As the head of department did not want to act as mentor, it simply fell to me as second-in-department.' This kind of imposition is obviously the worst case, but it does dramatize the potential vulnerability of a student teacher in a school-based scheme, especially given that the mentor in question will have the main say in passing or failing such a student (see Chapter 5). What if the English department has an excellent mentor but she leaves part way through the year? What if three departments in one school have excellent mentors but it becomes increasingly clear that a fourth has a poor one and that the affected students are turning to everyone else for advice and support, even the mentors of other subject areas?

This spotlight on the increased importance of mentorship illuminates how much is expected of the person in that role and also how little accountability there may be if the role, for whatever reason, is filled badly.

A second major concern about school-based teacher education is the nature of the teachers it is educating. There are many differing and quite oppositional views about what teachers do, and I shall discuss in detail later the concept of the reflective practitioner (Chapters 3 and 6), but here it is enough to point out that teachers themselves have conflicting views about the nature of teaching. Whether they would use the term or not, these are theories of teaching. Many teachers, in a staff room exchange for example, will sum up their philosophy quite succinctly. Over a period of years I asked my student teachers to jot down phrases that teachers had used that they had found memorable. Here is a selection from the list: 'teachers aren't made, they are born,' 'it's all about acting, convincing them that you know everything,' 'it's personality, you have to have lots of personality,' 'you have to be entertaining, make them laugh and you've got them on your side,' 'it's sink or swim,' 'you can't learn about teaching in books, you just do it until you can do it well,' 'never smile until Christmas and then start not smiling again in January,' 'it's all about trust, once they trust you, you can do anything,' 'show them who is the boss and then remind them at least once every lesson' and so on.

Any experienced teacher is likely to recognize these phrases; they are what has been called 'teachers' lore',[4] the typical kinds of folk sayings that circulate in a profession. Like all such sayings they are both cliché and wisdom. For a student teacher they are at best thought provoking and at worst utterly confusing. They are also said for a reason; the speaker is making a point and it is no accident that the receiver is a student teacher.

The use of such sayings is hardly new, but student teachers' spending of two-thirds of their formative experience among them does change the situational dynamics. This might be expressed via the good old pendulum: will the swing to school-based teacher education mean far too much practice and not enough theory? To use a different kind of terminology, will there be too much simplistic imitation by student teachers and not enough genuine learning? How many teachers are good at teaching adults to become teachers of children?

For example, most English teachers agree that English is a very difficult subject to define and that everyone has to come to terms with it (see Chapter 2), but how will student teachers come to terms with it if they have little chance to think about it? Whatever the faults of previous systems, they certainly offered lots of opportunities for thinking and talking, and reading and writing, about English in an educational context. This intellectual element has, *potentially*, been severely reduced. It used to be provided very efficiently. You put a considerable number of student teachers of English in a room together and made them all think at the same time. Now, it might be said, you scatter them among geographically distant schools and you leave it to one particular mentor figure to replace all that 'intellectual' loss. I am over-stating the case somewhat, but not over-emphasizing the potential effect. How can a mentor, whose main job is teaching children, find the time to keep up-to-date and knowledgeable herself about a fast changing subject and communicate this to one or possibly two adult learners in an effective way? I believe that she can, to an extent, but it is much more likely that the HEI tutor will be, if nothing else, more experienced and more proficient at this element of teacher educa-tion. In my experience, mentors are very clear and even more supportive of the HEI element than they ever were, and this is a strength in partnership. However, another issue that deserves attention at this stage relates to change of a different kind. A good mentor may indeed be up-to-date and highly aware of the best practice but, even so, every school differs, quite rightly, in its emphasis and its concerns. A student teacher is not being educated *for that school* or even for that moment. A student teacher, under current legislation, is receiving her one and only period dedicated to learning about teaching in a systematic way; she is being educated for *any school and for future schools*. The pace of change is such that a teacher education course has to identify stable elements that will underpin and provide a foundation for a student teacher wherever she takes her first post, while simultaneously giving her access to skills that we know she will need.

Information technology (IT) is always the most striking example. We know that the majority of current English teachers feel very under-trained in the use of IT,[5] both personally and for classroom work with children. However, stu-dent teachers, in general, are very positive about IT and keen to use it in the classroom. For many there is almost no opportunity to do so because some departments rarely use it. The student might go to a job interview and be rejected for a lack of familiarity with IT had she not had some chance to explore its potential on the HE part of the course. I might make similar points about media education and about drama, aspects of English that are increasingly important but that currently are represented, sometimes under-represented, in very different ways in different departments.

There is evidence that many teachers now think that the move to school-based teacher education has gone far enough, perhaps even a little too far. Many teachers, mentors in particular, are concerned that there is not enough time for student teachers to think about English teaching, especially in these newer and challenging areas. Most thinking professionals welcome the notion of new ideas, and particularly when enthusiastic novices wish to try them out but need the support of an 'old hand', especially the kind of 'old hand' that wants to stay fresh and recognizes a learning opportunity when she sees one. As one mentor put the advantage of the role for her: 'The main benefit is the stimulus provided by having to relate to people new to the profession – stu-dents bring new and fresh ideas, they have new eyes to help us to see clearly again.' We need, then, a partnership concept of the intellectual dimension. There is a real danger that school-based may become *school-only* teacher edu-cation, with none of the advantages that the HE dimension currently provides.

For many reasons, then, the mentor role in school is now of tremendous importance and it is a far more sophisticated role than the one envisaged by those who simply legislated to move teacher education into schools. It is per-sonally and professionally demanding and it is a role that we are still exploring and developing. One mentor summed up its demands on him:

The main benefit of being a subject mentor is that one tends to review and scrutinize one's own practice more regularly and in greater depth and detail. Having a student puts a high premium on personal practice – as a head of department, I suppose there is more to lose in a professional sense if things go wrong. As a result of being a mentor I feel that I am far more critical of my own practice; again, the role has created an opportunity for personal and professional development. On the down side, however, there are several factors. Students are emotionally quite draining: following negative experiences the onus is on the mentor to rebuild confidence, suggest ways forward, and generally pick up the pieces. This, squeezed in between year 7 and year 9, in the middle of the afternoon, is often quite traumatic for both parties.

I hope that the rest of the book will acknowledge all the up and down sides of mentoring and will provide some support for those who are, or who are thinking of, wrestling with the task.

2 Coming to terms with 'English': student teachers, mentors and the subject of English

Teaching? No problem

I shall begin this chapter with an examination of a crucial paradox. There are two groups of people to whom teaching appears relatively unproblematic. The first group are the highly experienced and successful teachers of English who are likely to be mentors, and the second group are student teachers at the beginning of their course.

This second group has, after all, many years of school 'experience' as a pupil and has decided that becoming an English teacher will be a satisfying and valuable career. The members of the group have spent some considerable time thinking about becoming teachers and, despite lots of advice from others that they should not go into teaching, for a whole host of reasons, they have still decided to go ahead. Some of this negative advice will even have come from experienced teachers, who have said, to the aforesaid prospective teachers, probably on a pre-PGCE interview visit to a school, that they should think of another, less stressful and more financially rewarding career. This advice is often delivered with a smile and then some kind of disavowal ('I don't really mean it, actually it is a great job'), but most prospective student teachers encounter such advice often enough to remark on it at their subsequent interview. Many have been genuinely shocked by such remarks; this is typical of that over-sensitivity described in Chapter 1. So these people, despite all the warnings, are still keen to become English teachers. After all they have appropriate degrees, they feel that the love of their subject is a permanent and lasting element in their lives and they are very willing to learn. The position statements that PGCE English student teachers write begin almost universally with a statement of a profound love of the subject, usually with special reference to literature. For example:

I have a love of the subject which I intend to be an infectious part of my teaching.

I have an enthusiasm for the 'subject', a love of literature and of my language.

I will bring a love of words and literature and a complete dedication to the subject.

I have a passion for literature and a love of words.

Finally, they feel reasonably sure that a PGCE course, despite all the 'theory bits', will turn them into good English teachers.

The experienced teachers have very different reasons for seeing teaching as relatively unproblematic. First, they have been 'doing it for years', they feel thoroughly at ease with children and have a vast reservoir of experience upon which to draw. Second, they tend to feel that they learnt most about teaching by 'doing it' and that their own PGCE course, or its equivalent, was a small step in their long journey into becoming highly accomplished. Third, and most important, because they are highly accomplished, most of what they do in the classroom has become *habitual* and, apparently, *intuitive*. They do not appear to plan with great care or even to write down lesson plans, yet in the classroom they effortlessly comprehend what is going on, and problems rarely occur because they see the signs well ahead of the problem developing.

Let us take, as an example,[1] Angela, a student teacher in her first week of observation, for whom it all still looks really easy. She is watching her mentor, Joyce, take a lesson. Joyce, a highly experienced and excellent teacher, on the way from the English office to the classroom, has already apologized to Angela because it will be such an ordinary lesson. She does not really plan much these days and has had no time to plan anything special for Angela, and so hopes she will not be bored.

The children are already attentive when Joyce begins the lesson, and they move smoothly from her initial explanation to group work on a poem. Moving furniture quickly and without fuss, they discuss the work with maturity and sensitivity, reporting back to the rest of the class about their interpretations. Minutes later they are busy writing their own poems and are eager to read each other's work and to gain their teacher's approval. All this time Joyce has moved quietly around the room, apparently chatting to pupils, and moving, without fuss or noise, one child who was a little distracted. As the class is concluded the children leave, commenting on how they enjoyed the lesson and hoping to do similar work tomorrow. The student teacher and the experienced teacher chat on the way to the staff room, the novice commenting on how much she enjoyed the lesson and confessing, with a laugh, how she wanted to write a poem herself. Joyce smiles and says modestly, 'Oh, they are such a nice class and they love poetry anyway.' Angela makes a mental note to ask to work with that class later, and looks forward to doing some poetry with them. After all, it looks so easy. Three months later she may have a very different view of that class and of teaching poetry in particular. Angela may also feel rather betrayed. It all looked so easy: why has no one told her the secret? There must be a secret because she knows that some teachers have it and others, like her, cannot seem to find it.

Unfortunately for Angela, she will have to find that 'secret' herself, although, paradoxically, it is in front of her nose. Part of it can only be found in classrooms, but there are many other places where useful pieces of the puzzle can be pieced together. The genial chat in the corridor, however well meant, was of no use to Angela whatsoever, and, in fact, she might have some justification later on for feeling frustrated. I would have to say that my impression, over the years, is that casual corridor comments, however well intentioned, have done more to confuse and, on occasion, profoundly upset student teachers than all their difficult Friday afternoon lessons put together. Such comments are generally aimed at the student teacher's own, recent, lesson, and tend to begin, 'That went quite well but you should have . . .', and by the time the pair have reached the staffroom the lesson has sunk, in the student's eyes, without trace. Naturally, I shall return to this area later in an appropriately systematic way. However, someone might also point out that Angela should have asked some searching questions: why, for example, did Joyce move that child? How did she organize such successful groups? How was the feedback to the whole class set up? How did she manage the transition from reading to writing with such ease? But we know that for Joyce it was an 'easy' lesson and to Angela it certainly looked like an easy one. Angela, as yet, does not know what to look for, never mind what to ask about.

The paradox that teaching looks easy to the experienced teacher who is now *unconsciously* competent and to the student who is unconsciously *incompetent* is a powerful one, and this book attempts to resolve it for teachers who want to be more than successful classroom teachers of English. For there is no doubt that being a good mentor does mean doing much more than letting student teachers watch you teach. There is no more reason to presume that Joyce will automatically and suddenly became a good mentor than that she automatically or suddenly became a good teacher. Becoming a good teacher took her many years and involved many mistakes. Now that she no longer makes many and has mostly 'forgotten' those past mistakes, how can she help Angela through the many mistakes that she will inevitably make? At the same time, Joyce wants to ensure that the children themselves do not suffer from Angela's initially clumsy efforts to teach them.

The problem with 'English'

Much of this book will examine this highly complex issue, and part of the answer lies in starting where both Joyce and Angela started, with the subject of English. This is not a general book about developing good teachers through mentoring – there are other books which adopt a general approach[2] – this is a book that combines attention to the generic points about mentorship with very specific attention to English. It is a psychological truism that we all like, when it suits us, to stress our difference, our fundamental individuality, and at other times to emphasize how normal we are and therefore how like to others. English teachers do form a very distinctive group, and are quite self-conscious about their distinctiveness. In Protherough and Atkinson's excellent *The Making of English Teachers* (Protherough and Atkinson, 1991: Chapter 1) there is a detailed section entitled, 'What sort of animal is an English teacher?' The teachers of English surveyed were almost unanimous in saying that English teachers are different from other teachers: 36 per cent pointed to personal qualities, 28 per cent to personal attitudes and 37 per cent to different relationships with pupils (*ibid.*: 13). These findings echo the views of Margaret Mathieson in her classic study of English teaching, *The Preachers of Culture* (Mathieson, 1975), in which she comments on the almost unbearable weight of expectations placed upon the personality and knowledge of each English teacher. For the next few pages I shall examine this distinctiveness, with the main purpose of helping experienced English teachers to review the subject, particularly as it appears to student and beginning teachers.

I began the Introduction with an example of a PGCE interview at which the candidate emphasized her love of reading. It is worth remembering that for the vast majority of English student teachers, five of their most intellectually formative years were spent reading and writing about literature, two at A level and three for their degree. This concentration tends to build on an even longer apprenticeship as a keen and enthusiastic reader. The result is that such student teachers frequently comment, as exemplified above, on their 'love of reading', their 'love of literature', their wish to 'inspire children with a love of books' and so on.

A first point to consider is that, for the PGCE year in particular, this apparent fund of knowledge is of very little use or relevance. When students 'discover' this it can be quite a traumatic shock. Suddenly a whole library of resources vanishes. Equally, they find that most children are apparently not much good at 'appreciating' literature. The experienced teachers know differently. Children can gain a great deal from complex literature, and knowing a great deal about such literature puts the teacher in a strong position. However, the missing element is what is usefully, if inelegantly, called 'subject pedagogical knowledge'; that is, applying what you know to children's learning. Student teachers are often particularly bad at teaching 'great' literature because they bring absolutely the wrong model to the classroom. I can think of numerous occasions when a student teacher has shown off her knowledge by talking about some writer to a class and then said, 'Of course, you have heard of so and so haven't you?', to which the class, whether they have or not, chorus 'No'; if it is an A level group they look at their feet and feel shamefaced. The student teacher's prize possession, an academic understanding of literature, confuses her about children and her ability to teach. The examples of teaching she saw during her own degree course are certainly not models that she should generally wish to adopt.

In the USA particularly, there has been some very useful research into this concept of 'subject pedagogical knowledge' – that is, knowing what to do with subject knowledge to make it accessible and valuable to children and adolescents – and I feel it worth illustrating my point above with an extensive section from a very useful book about the teacher education of future English teachers, *The Making of a Teacher: Teacher Knowledge and Teacher Education* (Grossman, 1990). This example is not a perfect fit with the British context but, I think, all the more useful as a starting point for us in thinking about how certain models affect student teachers' thinking, because the differences between the two student teachers are more dramatic than we would tend to find. At the opening of the book she describes two student teachers whose work she closely monitored.

> Jake and Steven, both beginning English teachers, each decided to teach *Hamlet* to their senior English classes [seniors are equivalent to A level students in terms of age]. Jake spent seven weeks on the play. He wanted students to see the interconnections among the themes of the play and to learn the skills involved in textual analysis or, as Jake put it, *explication de texte*. Jake also wanted his students to understand the power and beauty of the play's language. During class, he led the students through the play, word by word, focusing particularly on the themes of linguistic reflexivity and the reflexivity of the play. His assignments included an in-class analysis of one soliloquy, memorisation and recitation of a soliloquy, a five-page paper on any theme of the play, and a final exam . . . Although he felt the students never fully appreciated the beauty of the play's language, Jake believed that by the end of the seven weeks they understood the themes of the play.
>
> Steven spent two-and-a-half weeks on the play. He wanted to help his students to see the connection between Hamlet's dilemmas and some of the dilemmas they might face in their own lives, and to pique students interest in the play and in Shakespeare. Steven began his unit on *Hamlet* without mentioning the play. Instead, he asked students how they might feel if their parents divorced and their mother suddenly started dating another man. After asking students to write about their responses to this situation, Steven 'introduced a new wrinkle': he told the students to imagine that their mother's new boyfriend had taken over their father's job and 'there's some talk that he had something to do with the ousting of your dad, and you can't quite prove it, but you sort of get that sense'. Again Steven asked the students to write about how they might feel. After this introduction, Steven asked his students to think about at what point they could imagine themselves killing another human being: the students again wrote their responses to this question.

Steven then introduced the play as a book 'about this guy and his family breaks up – he's confused and he doesn't know what to do.'

> During the unit, Steven showed parts of the videotape of the play, providing students with plot summaries, which they read prior to watching. In discussions

of the play, Steven tried to move back and forth between the play and the student's own experiences, 'to narrow the gap between Hamlet's problems and their problems.' During this time the students never read the play itself. In lieu of a final exam, Steven asked students to write an essay in which they chose a characteristic of Hamlet's and demonstrated how that characteristic existed in people today. Steven asked students to find evidence from the text that would support their arguments. The class spent about a week working on these papers, using class time to work in small groups to brainstorm and share ideas, and to organise and revise their first drafts. By the end of the unit, Steven felt that students responded enthusiastically to the themes regarding the family, although he worried that he had not spent sufficient time on the play itself.

(Grossman, 1990: 1–2)

Jake adopts a straight literature-as-appreciation model and Steven a personal growth mixed with reader response model (both of these are discussed below). One difference is that Steven has taken some English education courses and Jake went straight from college into school; in other words, Steven has been developing some subject pedagogical knowledge and reflecting on how to engage children's motivation and interest. Grossman's book does not suggest that the differences are as simple as they look. However, my point is that some student teachers that we may encounter will be exactly like Jake, in that their heads are full of literary models suited to undergraduate and postgraduate study but not to school children, even A level students. In the UK context all secondary English teachers must take the PGCE whether they like it or not, and so we can use the above example to remind us of the mutual job that we do in helping student teachers of English to escape from narrow and unreflective models of teaching.

Mixed in with the literary models are memories of those teachers who did switch future English teachers on to literature. Student teachers often recall inspiring and enthusiastic teachers of A level literature whose influence they still feel; in fact who are quite often a principal cause for their deciding to become an English teacher. But what is it that they are recalling? Is it their own transformation from ordinary adolescents into serious lovers of literature, or is it the methodology of the teachers in question?

For the student's mentor there is much valuable work to do in helping student teachers to come to terms with all these confusing personal memories and this curious loss of expertise. They have a whole new 'canon' to come to terms with, the English department canon. Certainly this canon has a relationship to the literary canon, but it is not a simple one. It is highly valuable for the mentor to gain a picture of the student teacher's literary background, and this is sure to play a part in her initial thinking about teaching English. It could mean that there is some expertise in literature that is of immediate use. If, for example, a student did her undergraduate dissertation on Thomas Hardy and a GCSE group is about to work on *Far from the Madding Crowd*, it might be appropriate to give the student that class. However, the mentor would have to do the reverse of what common sense would suggest and work extra hard to help the student get away from the mass of subject knowledge to the application of that knowledge to a GCSE class. The mentor might initially feel that a student's degree is just something to ask politely about and then to move on to the real business of teaching. However, for the student teacher this literary knowledge, combined with her unreliable memories of what inspirational literature teachers are like, are very powerful models that can either play a part or, more commonly, significantly interfere with her understanding of how to work with children. The example of Jake, above, is very striking here. This literary background is, for most student teachers, 'where they are coming from' and can help a mentor to understand that starting position and its very real limitations.

Another very significant and formative influence on most beginning English teachers is their more general 'love of reading', their long-term personal habit. Again, common sense would suggest that this must be a great advantage if you are going to try to instil the same habit in children, adolescents and young adults. However, there is plenty of evidence to show that student teachers generally have much to 'unlearn', and English student teachers have a specific problem with the reading habit. I shall examine this in some detail so that a mentor can think through how she would help a student teacher to stand back from what seems 'natural' and so see clearly what is in fact a construction.

The simplest point is that being a constant reader is not either typical or, even, particularly 'normal'. Despite the constant media rumblings and governmental complaints about falling reading standards, children do still read a great deal and enjoy what they read (see, for example, P. Benton, Children's reading and viewing in the nineties, in Davies, 1996). However, most children do not read anything like as much as student teachers of English remember that they read. My own work over a number of years has involved helping my student teachers to review their reading history. This helps them initially to recognize just how much they have read over the years; for most, actually learning to read was itself very straightforward, and again this is not representative of the population. For the great majority, their literal memories are of the intense pleasure and comfort of their earliest reading experiences; or they simply cannot remember how they learned. In either case, they need to reflect on the fact that only a few children in any class will be likely to bring such positive or unproblematic memories to reading.

A second consideration is that their reading history is actually more typical than they initially remembered. They tend to find, having made the conscious effort to recall their adolescence, that once they became teenagers they actually read far less than when younger; a fact that makes them similar to most adolescents. They also become aware that most of the books that they read in school at this stage – that is, Key Stages 3 and 4 – are not fondly remembered; frequently they cannot remember them at all. The books they do remember tend to be ones that they chose themselves; some of these texts were very powerful. This new understanding of themselves helps the student teachers to adjust some of their attitudes and expectations about children and about the nature of the challenge of teaching books to those children. All of these points are part of beginning the process of reflecting on teaching, but they begin, necessarily for the student with little teaching experience, by reflecting on the subject and her experiences of that subject.

A final and extremely important point, at least in my view, is that this autobiographical critique uncovers a strong undercurrent of guilt in their thinking. In looking back, student teachers often write about the dichotomy between what they 'had to read for work' and what they enjoyed reading 'for themselves'. The fact is that whatever the level of the work, from GCSE right up to masters level, they still found themselves secretly enjoying books that they describe as 'trashy', 'just popular', 'light weight', 'superficial' and so on. These comments often take the form of a confessional. There are powerful feelings of guilt connected to the straightforward enjoyment of reading as opposed to the study of important and valuable literature. I shall return to this point below.

For some student teachers, of whatever age, especially if they have come straight from a degree course, there is a powerful feeling of reading fatigue. They feel that they never wish to read 'like that' again. Despite their literary expertise, discussed above, there is a counter feeling of personal damage. They look back on aspects of their literary training as ruinous of enjoyment. Poetry in particular was 'dissected', 'torn apart', 'taken apart', and they feel strongly that they never want to repeat that approach with their future classes. However, as I have tried to show with the examples above, they are very likely to do just that because they have experienced that model so intensely, and over the past several years they have often unconsciously internalized this approach. It cannot be seen for what it is, until it can be seen.

Student teachers of English then, can be experiencing a difficult inner struggle, not always at a conscious level, about the value of reading. They have a problem to work through. They have kept their 'love of books' often *despite* their literary training. Some of their degree work was profoundly exciting and satisfying, but much of it was 'work' in the negative sense of drudgery. This is highly problematic for someone who says that she 'loves reading'. Equally, as I discussed above, they have learned to feel guilty about reading anything that is 'not worthy'. Often then, the reading that was straightforwardly enjoyable did not count as real reading, it was not work. Any reader can see that this is a complicated and somewhat messy state of mind; even more so if they accept my view that often this is operating subconsciously and is more related to feelings than a thought through and considered point of view.

I am suggesting that a mentor has a powerful role to play in helping student teachers of English to come to terms with a whole range of issues related to the values surrounding the apparently straightforward term 'reading'. At a simple level this means that just discussing what you, an experienced English teacher, like to read, and somehow find time for, is a helpful strategy. It is not solely about getting to know a particular human being, but it is also a way of helping student teachers to articulate and come to terms with this 'messy state of mind'. For example, student teachers of English often do 'fall back' on very literary models of teaching, especially when teaching poetry. So their own memories of poems being 'ruined' for them seem to disappear as they drag reluctant children through a poem trawling for metaphors and similes like so many fish. The result of this trawl is usually quite a catch of slippery phrases that then have to be thrown back in the poem without anyone benefiting much. For a mentor the temptation might be to focus solely on the fact that she has just witnessed some rather mediocre teaching, but there is another dimension which takes some getting at and which I am suggesting is worth the effort. Gradually, student teachers of English need to recognize where their literary training *interferes with* their developing subject pedagogical knowledge. This interference, being frequently deep down, needs careful and even constant attention. Using this example once more, it would be helpful for the student to discuss the point of reading poetry and also her memories of enjoyable poetry sessions. The student teacher might be puzzled and simply want to know 'how to do it better next time', and there will be plenty to say on that point too. The confusions that the student teacher feels may well be inexplicable without some attention to what is going on behind her surface attention to a poetry lesson.

If student English teachers have difficulty with literature teaching, this is partly caused, as we noted above, by the lack of fit between some of their personal experiences and their literary training. They do not feel a lack of *knowledge*. What induces far more anxiety in such teachers is, as they perceive it, their ignorance about language, sometimes narrowly defined as 'grammar'. Generally they are adamant that they learnt nothing about this in their own schooling, and several years of intensive study of some of the best known works in the language have not provided them with any useful understanding of 'how language actually works'. They often express their fear of being caught out by children who might innocently ask about, for example, what a past participle is. With language then, the problem tends to be the opposite to literature: the student teacher feels ignorant and has a very active wish to acquire linguistic knowledge. This actually puts a mentor in a more straightforward and positive position. The current teacher education year is so busy that there is no time for a course in such linguistic knowledge.

As an aside it is worth remembering that the Kingman Report (DES, 1988: 70–1) recommended strongly that university English departments should provide more language courses for future English teachers. It is also very relevant to remember that the Language in the National Curriculum project was effectively curtailed by a ministerial decision, removing from schools the materials that might have been of great use to student teachers in this respect.

To return to the mentor's role, I am suggesting that the student is not likely to find that her anxieties about her lack of language expertise can easily be resolved through her higher education course element. I am not suggesting, however, that this puts the mentor in sole charge of a student teacher's linguistic knowledge. In fact, the mentor's sympathetic awareness of this anxiety can, in itself, provide a great deal of help. A particularly useful strategy here involves giving the student teacher a sense of perspective about acquiring the kinds of linguistic knowledge that will be useful when working with children. Most English teachers learned their own linguistic knowledge *through their teaching*, and so student teachers should not expect too much of themselves in this respect. Equally, like the children they will be teaching, they know a great deal more than they think they do. Mentors may sometimes have to talk through with their student teachers their own learning about language, in this way reviewing and revisiting the difficulties of their own acquisition and also reassuring students about what is reasonably to be expected of a beginning teacher.

Where is English coming from?

As described above, student English teachers bring their own, very powerful memories of their schooling in English to their initial encounters with children and teachers. Student teachers' own period in school may have been as little as three years previously, or as many as thirty or so ago. Essentially the time scale is of small importance: the issue of perception is of great importance. I will not waste the time of readers of this book with a detailed account of the innumerable changes that the school subject of English has undergone in the past few years[3] but I do think it valuable to bear these changes in mind as we focus on this idea of the student teacher's perceptions about that subject.

As a starting point it might seem too obvious to state that a student teacher's perception of what 'English' means is based mostly on vague memories of what she enjoyed and valued at school. Often these values are defined negatively: 'I certainly never intend to use sarcasm in the classroom to reject a child's view of a book,' 'I will never force children to like a poem' and so on. What is crucial for a mentor is the recognition of the range of forces at work on a student teacher's thinking. It is worth stating these clearly.

A student teacher is open to new ideas and to old ideas. It is inevitable that some of the 'new' ideas about English teaching are coming from the higher education tutors that the students work with. This is not to suggest that these tutors are the only source of such ideas, but to the student teacher they may seem so for two powerful reasons. First, there is an expectation, genuinely felt by teachers in school, as well as student teachers themselves, that the job of higher education tutors is to provide such ideas. Therefore, when the mood is positive, this factor is constantly identified as one of the key reasons for higher education to be involved in teacher education. This 'access to new ideas', this 'keeping up to date', is highly rated by departments that regularly work with a higher education institution. However, when the mood is negative, new ideas may become 'theory', something not really tried and tested, something to be wary of and to be seen as created by people who 'are a bit out of touch'. This is a difficult mixed message.

The second difficulty is that many 'new' ideas will have been experienced by student teachers when they were taught, but that is not what the *then pupil* experienced. It was not a new idea then, it was simply what went on in the classroom and 'worked'. When under pressure, student teachers fall back, frequently unconsciously, to patterns of teaching that are definitely not 'new', because deep in the British psyche, in my opinion, is a powerful notion that teaching is principally about control and wearing a mortar board and a gown. Student teachers are then likely to fall back to narrow ways of teaching that they may, actually, never have directly experienced. In other words, student teachers are inevitably confused about notions of 'old' and 'new', 'progressive' and 'traditional'. A mentor is therefore placed in a key mediating role. As students struggle to make sense of what they perceive to be, 'new' ideas, they need a great deal of help with assimilating such ideas, and a consistency of approach from the higher education tutors and the school mentors can tremendously help a student teacher.

These subject memories and perceptions are present in the thinking of student teachers of whatever subject. However, English has proved itself time and again the most controversial and contested secondary school subject. Again, the higher education element of the course can orientate student teachers towards an understanding of why English is so controversial and of the general changes which have been made to its shape in school over the past few years. In that sense at least, student teachers are brought up to date. However, when this is placed in conjunction with some of the disturbing confusions described above, we see that for student teachers of English there is real danger of confusion overload. 'Theory' will come up many times in this book, but for me, at least, theory means how we understand, how we make sense of things, how, in fact, we answer the question 'why?' In the case of English, the recent (and indeed entire) history of the subject simply cannot be understood without asking 'but why?' because changes cannot be explained as innocent or neutral. I mentioned above the curtailment of the Language in the National Curriculum project.[4] How can this be explained without exposing vastly different theories of what English teaching is for?

In this very practical way, then, student teachers have to make some sense of what is going on. Their attention, inevitably, is with what we might call the foreground; that is, what is happening right now, perhaps in the next lesson they will have to teach. The background, say changes to coursework or the introduction of SATs for all children, may seem rather remote from the concerns of even the next year 9 class. In one sense, student teachers are incapable of taking in all these bewildering changes to English, given their limited ability at this stage of their teaching to take in very much (see Chapter

3). However, what they certainly do need, as we all tend to do, is coherence. In this respect we are looking at the underlying principles of English teaching and some understanding of why English teachers do what they do and also, at times, why they espouse one approach but 'have' to use a different one.

We are returning to the idea of development and to what is practically helpful in ensuring development. There are problems making sense of the messy confusion of English teaching for the most experienced teacher or tutor. Given that a student teacher can have strong personal convictions about the subject and powerful, but perhaps inaccurate, or potentially misleading memories of what English is or was like, how can she make sense of all that is going on? One way to make sense is through articulating beliefs about English teaching, and most of us find this much more productive in dialogue. There will be some of this dialogue in the higher education element of the course, and there such dialogue has a constant, challenging function; it is part of the 'new ideas' notion.

But how, amidst all this controversy, does English actually 'work'? One mentor expressed her own problems with defining the subject:

> There's the whole National Curriculum debate anyway about what is the canon and what is of value, and it's a big crisis in English studies anyway, not just in schools but at university level. What do you teach? What is a text? I mean for me it's not a debate I've ever resolved. Why do you think Shakespeare is better than, I don't know, Catherine Cookson or whatever, but you know – I would say that that's my main aim – stimulating a love of literature. But also, I mean, one of the problems with English is that you can see it in so many ways – and use it as a study skills type subject, and there's more of an emphasis on that.
>
> (Dart and Drake, 1996)

In this study, by Dart and Drake, there is a great deal of evidence of a powerful need for mentors and student teachers to step back from the approaching impact of the next lesson and to review what is going on beneath the surface, in order to help student teachers to make sense of what is going on. Mentors who take an appropriately long-term view of a student teacher's development will know that the diversity of English teaching means that a successful, effective teacher of English will have gradually and thoughtfully absorbed a broad understanding of what 'works'. That broad understanding is an absolutely invaluable resource for the student teacher, and is at least as developmental as a neat piece of discrete advice about how to orchestrate a poetry sequencing activity. What, after all, is the point of cutting up a poem just to put it back together again? The point comes from a broad understanding of how pupils engage with text, poetic text in particular.

Any successful mentor creates a relationship where there is a shared understanding of purpose for the mentee. Any student teacher has what might be called an emergent rationale for her teaching. This is still true of all of us, particularly those who try to continue in their own development. In that sense, then, the student teacher, perhaps unconsciously, wants to be 'like us'. Her constant questioning is simply that drive to gain some purchase on why things are happening the way they are. It is clearly not enough for a student teacher to encounter discussions about theories of English in conversations with other student teachers of English. I am not suggesting that current mentors of English students do not do this already, I know that many do. However, they are always struggling with time:

> What's difficult in your mentor time is having enough time if you like to debate philosophy rather than pragmatics – and a lot of the time we spent discussing the lessons, what happened in the lessons and why, rather than if you like the philosophy behind them, simply because of the pressure of time. So thinking back on my mentorship last year that was something that was missing. In a sense I tended to feel well perhaps the university was doing that – I tend to leave the philosophy in a sense out and tend to concentrate on this worked, this didn't work.
>
> (Dart and Drake, 1996: 63)

In fact, English teachers do not really leave the philosophy out because it informs all their judgements, and this is where the issue of dialogue is so crucial. Dart and Drake found that when mentors were talking about what they valued in English teachers some made comments like:

> I suppose the bottom line for me, because we are a literature based department and I've always chosen to work in literature orientated departments, was a sensitivity to literature and a deep understanding of that, and it's, you know the things that go into making a work of literature, and the ability to recognise and separate out those component parts, like character and plot, and above all a sort of sensitivity to language, particularly when you're dealing with poetry.
>
> (*Ibid.*: 67)

Others were even more straightforward in their definitions of what they expected in an English teacher. Here are three different mentors' comments.

> I think it is somebody who, who is really interested in texts and can actually convey that enthusiasm for the written material to pupils, and also in terms of writing as well, a real genuine love of literature.

> So a good English teacher has got to be able to enjoy reading and be able to communicate not only a love of literature but knowledge about how certain aspects and qualities of that literature have been achieved.

> Obviously a love of subject and a love of literature in particular.
>
> (*Ibid.*: 72–3)

In all these views we can trace the predominantly Leavisite mode of English teaching. In Chris Davies's study of the attitudes and values of English teachers in the mid-1980s (Davies, 1996), he found overwhelmingly that the majority of teachers were very much in the liberal humanist, Leavisite position. In my own small scale piece of research in the late 1980s (Goodwyn, 1992a), I found very much the same, although with some real sense of some change (see the next section). The key point is that for both student teachers and mentors the power of subject beliefs is especially important, and may heavily influence the mentor's judgements of the quality of teaching. This is one reason why a competency model is important, because it lays out an agreed framework; this will be discussed at more length in Chapter 5. I am suggesting then that a more planned and coherent approach to considering subject beliefs and attitudes is an important element in a mentor's work with students. The next section examines one framework for such an approach.

Student teachers of English and models of English

In 1989 the Cox Report (DES, 1989) identified five models of English that the Cox committee suggested were present in secondary school English and that all English teachers would recognize. The Cox definitions are as follows.

A *personal growth* view focuses on the child: it emphasizes the relationship between language and learning in the individual child, and the role of literature in developing children's imaginative and aesthetic lives.

A *cross-curricular* view focuses on the school: it emphasizes that all teachers have a responsibility to help children with the language demands of different subjects in the school curriculum; otherwise areas of the curriculum may be closed to them. In England, English is different from other school subjects, in that it is both a subject and a medium of instruction for other subjects.

An *adult needs* view focuses on communication outside the school: it emphasizes the responsibility of English teachers to prepare children for the language of adult life, including the workplace in a fast-changing world. Children need to learn to deal with the day-to-day demands of spoken language and of print; they also need to be able to write clearly, appropriately and effectively.

A *cultural heritage* view emphasizes the responsibility of schools to lead children to an appreciation of those works of literature that have been widely regarded as among the finest in the language.

A *cultural analysis* view emphasizes the role of English in helping children towards a critical understanding of the world and cultural environment in which they live. Children should know about the processes by which meanings are conveyed, and about the ways in which print and other media carry values.

Subsequent research (Goodwyn, 1992a) has shown this picture to have been a somewhat inaccurate sketch. English teachers do not, for example, recognize the cross-curricular model as a model of English. They do, however, see it as a key model of learning that is of relevance to all teachers. They are quite clear that this model belongs to the whole school and should not be identified with English. If it does, it becomes self-defeating, as its actual purpose is clearly to help teachers of other subjects to pay proper attention to the language that they use and that they encourage children to use.

The other four models are acknowledged as a normal part of English, but they do not have a comfortable or neutral relationship with each other; neither are they politically or historically innocent, they are not simply 'there'. To sum up a good deal of complex research, the majority of English teachers espouse personal growth as their *raison d'être*, with cultural analysis and adult needs coming closely second and third. This is not to suggest that English teachers, experienced ones in particular, think that an individual lesson is one model or another. It is mainly a matter of emphasis and of shifting attention. For example, a lesson looking at advertising may well be addressing the language development and personal views of each child (personal growth), the needs of the class when older to make sense of advertising (adult needs) and the critical skills of each individual to deconstruct and recognize the codes of advertising (cultural analysis). Even this explanation over-simplifies the very complex learning processes that a skilful English teacher will be encouraging. However, cultural heritage will mainly be missing from such a lesson because it is so closely associated with the study of literature and of 'classic' literature in particular. In another lesson, perhaps teaching the pre-twentieth century literature requirement of the National Curriculum, it may be absolutely pre-eminent.

In general terms, English teachers are increasingly uneasy with the cultural heritage model, especially as it has been given, in their views, far too much weight in the National Curriculum. This discomfort has nothing to do with their continuing, passionate attachment to literature, but everything to do with the increasing antithesis between cultural heritage and personal growth. Student teachers are not joining a professional group at a time of stability and consolidation; they are entering something of a fray and a ferment.

My own, ongoing research with student teachers of English reveals an even more dramatic perspective on the models. Their espousal of personal growth is almost universal; no other model comes close. However, cultural analysis comes in second place and, over the period of their initial teacher education course, increases in support. Student teachers of English are even more emphatic in their rejection of cultural heritage, and many of these have only just finished either three or five years of literary study; in fact, this may explain their rejection!

However, as described above, their espousal of such models is not the same as their teaching, in terms of either its conception and planning or its execution. A student teacher may therefore be trying very hard to adopt a personal growth approach but, in fact, fall back on teaching a very cultural heritage lesson. For example, the student may want to have children working out and interpreting a poem through group work and classroom discussion, an approach stemming from reader response theory, but, in actuality, teach a lesson in which the children are, eventually, taken through a critical appreciation of a 'masterpiece'. There will be many elements in this confusion of intention and purpose and the mistakes being made are, in a sense, quite normal parts of learning to teach English.

From the mentor's point of view it may be vitally important to help the student teacher to recognize where some of these confusions are coming from; in a way they are a result of forces external to the student. In examining these forces, the mentor is not dealing with irrelevant or abstract theories about English, but with powerful forces that affect teachers and children in very ordinary, everyday ways.

There is much to be said for discussing at least some lessons by using the models as a starting point. The student teacher can often see some of the trees, but it is the mentor that knows the wood. Even then, the interaction with the student may help the mentor to see the wood much more clearly than when she has her eyes down on the normal pathway of a tiring day. As student and mentor look up together at the whole picture, some of the parts will actually be clearer. Student teachers very frequently recount English lessons that they have taught, with the mentor observing, that the mentor feels strongly *did not actually happen*. Student teachers are not pretending, they are simply stuck behind one of those proverbial trees. If the mentor, for at least a part of discussions, can ask the student to stand back and analyse what went on in terms of the models, then it becomes possible to discuss issues of coherence and explicitness. It also helps to direct criticism away from the student teacher and towards quite normal, external shaping forces that the experienced mentor also has to struggle with. It is worth reiterating that this is especially important for teachers dealing with English, a subject that shows no sign of 'settling down' for some time yet, or perhaps ever.

To return to the poetry lesson above, it is likely that the student teacher has not thought through the teacher's role in a reader response style lesson. This is unsurprising, because the teacher's role is so subtle in such situations; so subtle as perhaps to appear, to a student teacher, practically invisible. In my experience, in response style lessons, student teachers of English often start interfering with the children's responses because they have not learned to trust this approach and also because they are fairly weak at monitoring class behaviour through systematic observation. Experienced teachers are excellent at this, but do it in very unobtrusive ways. The student's inexperience often leads to a messy lesson where the children did not have long enough to develop a response and then become rather bored and resentful as she points out all the things they 'missed' in the poem. A mentor's intervention here should not start with 'You should have given them longer to talk', which may well reinforce in the student a view that such approaches 'don't work for me' and bring out that defensiveness that interferes with learning. Instead, the feedback might begin with a general question about the student's view of how children get better at understanding poems, leading then into a recognition that the plan was sound and that next time the student teacher might experiment with giving the class longer to make some interpretations, comparing that experience with the recent one.

As well as helping student teachers of English to make sense of what they see in experienced teacher's classrooms and of the messier events in their own, this attention to what English is 'all about' helps them with their broader awareness of the profession. As described in Chapter 1, students usually get some experience in two schools, but most courses base a student for a great majority of the time in one school. As the time in the HEI education institution is much reduced, this does lessen students' contacts with each other and also their awareness of what other English departments are like. Tutors and mentors are usually aware of this and can make efforts to overcome the limitations of the situation. However, a great deal is expected of a beginning teacher of English and this includes when she tries to get a job.

In an interview, some questions focus on knowledge, some on awareness but, overall, a display of interviewee coherence is vital. Interviewers frequently apply what can only be described as the 'bullshit' test to any candidate, and this stems from ordinary human concerns about sincerity and authenticity. A mentor is important not just in helping a student teacher with hints about 'interview technique' or 'typical questions' but in being able to articulate a rationale for her approach to English.

So far, although I have mentioned that each student teacher is very much an individual, I have also looked in a very general way at typical issues that normally affect student teachers of English; for example, their 'love of reading' factor. I am quite certain that these general issues are the norm and will impinge on the initial teaching efforts of almost any student teacher of English. However, being a student of English does not necessarily mean the same thing to many people. A mentor might be quite shocked to find out that her student teacher, who happens to have a very good degree from a famous university, has not studied Shakespeare since A level. In fact, this is a reasonably common occurrence and bears no relationship to the ability of the mentee either as a student or as a potential teacher. What it usefully emphasizes is that the possession of an English degree does not offer much uniformity, and mentors are well advised not to expect it. If anything, the personal and subjective elements associated with English, at school and at degree level, may have accentuated differences between students in all kinds of ways. Looked at in this way, any mentor can recognize the need to balance some planned interventions with all students with some diagnostic discussions that help to fine tune a programme to help an individual. A mentor can quite usefully begin this process by simply acknowledging that an English degree can be very different from one institution to another, and so can legitimately enquire what a student feels that she knows about the subject.

Student teachers and reflective practice

Whatever the individual differences between student teachers of English in terms of their subject knowledge, background or personality, one thing obviously unites them, and that is their wish to become good teachers. However,

I have already touched a number of times on the student teachers' perception that they are frequently the victims of conflicting advice. How can they make sense of conflicting advice and of the messy reality of the classroom, with its infinite and frequently unpredictable variables? What they need, I would argue, is the mental flexibility to accommodate such difficulties and to turn them, as with my earlier analogy with the novelist, into useful material. They also need a vision of development that is not linked solely to their initial year's training course or to their first year of induction (supposing they receive a proper induction), but to a concept of continuing professional and personal development (see Chapters 5 and 6).

The concept of the reflective practitioner is one that achieves this aim and has been widely discussed and increasingly supported over the past twenty years. The idea of the reflective practitioner starts from the premise that people who choose a profession are selecting more than a mere career path, they are choosing a *way of being* which involves them in a constant search for improving their practice within that professional pathway. A mentor needs to consider a number of issues in relation to reflective practice. If she accepts this concept, then how is she to help a student to begin to be a reflective practitioner? Does she feel that the concept fits her own approach to her professional work? Finally, and this comes up importantly in Chapter 6, is she going to contribute to the profession by being a role model as a reflective practitioner? These are all important issues, but for now I am going to concentrate on looking at the concept in relation to student teachers themselves, beginning with the best known, recent work on this idea.

Donald Schön, picking up on the pioneering work of John Dewey at the beginning of the century, is the most prominent figure in the development of the concept and his work is sufficiently well known for me to provide some further reading references in the notes at this point[5] and to concentrate here on my use of the concept. In Chapter 6 I shall look at his ideas in more depth. I am defining a reflective practitioner as someone who reflects systematically on her practice in a constant attempt to improve it. This makes it clear that such reflection is not only a conscious action but also a deliberate choice. A practitioner can certainly improve just through what appears to be practice and experience, partly because it seems that some reflection is common to almost all human activity. The reflective practitioner, however, is operating at a much higher and more critical level, having recognized that some aspects of experience lead to an inability to challenge and question our received assumptions. The reflective practitioner has thus become the model that teacher educators tend to offer for all their students and they are now attempting to enshrine the principles of reflective practice in their courses.

However, there has been a great deal more recent discussion about the idea that student teachers are not capable of much genuine reflective practice during their training year. Donald McIntyre (McIntyre *et al.*, 1993) in particular has argued this point. In 1980 McIntyre began this discussion, and Alexander moved it forward by focusing first on an attempt to define what theory should mean in relation to initial teacher education. Alexander summed up McIntyre's view as:

a continual process of hypothesis testing framed by a detailed analysis of the values and practical constraints fundamental to teaching. The 'theory' for teacher education should therefore incorporate, (i) speculative theory, (ii) the findings of empirical research, (iii) the craft knowledge of practising teachers; but none should be presented as having prescriptive implications for practice: instead students should be encouraged to approach their own practice with the intention of testing hypothetical principles drawn from the consideration of these different types of knowledge.

(Alexander *et al.*, 1984)

McIntyre (1993) accepts this summary but places much more emphasis now on the practical value of theory, defining it as a theory with real 'content'. I would express this simply as ideas that help student teachers to learn how to teach. We wish them to develop their own ideas and to challenge received wisdom, but they will necessarily have to begin with at least some of that wisdom in order to make an informed start.

McIntyre goes on to argue that it is only really experienced teachers who are genuinely able to learn as reflective practitioners. Student teachers need to depend on others.

For the novice who needs to develop ways of construing situations and possibilities for effective action within these situations, there is a necessary dependence on ideas from sources outside his or her own teaching experiences. These *may* be their experiences in other kinds of context, but more usefully in most cases they will be ideas gained from working with experienced teachers, from tutors or from reading; and, being ideas which are not rooted in their own experience, they will tend initially to be used less fluently and less flexibly.

This dependence places the mentor, like the tutor, in a key position. The students' limited range of reflection mainly tends to help them to identify that they need assistance from a range of sources. So, McIntyre argues, reflection is of limited value to them for their own learning but 'learning to reflect must surely be an important *goal* for student teachers, since it is through reflection on their own teaching that they will increasingly with experience be able to continue learning.'

McIntyre suggests that there may be three levels of theorizing and reflecting. The first, *technical*, level is concerned with the effective attainment of given goals. With the second, *practical*, level the concern is with the assumptions, predispositions, values and consequences with which the actions are linked. At the third, *critical or emancipatory*, level the concern includes wider ethical, social and political issues, including, crucially, the institutional and societal forces which may constrain the individual's freedom of action or limit the efficacy of his or her actions. McIntyre feels that student teachers need to focus on level one for a considerable time before moving on to the challenge of level two. The third, most sophisticated, level can, and should, be explored with them, but not in relation to their own practice, which is not sufficiently established for students to be truly reflective. Instead, students should be helped to reflect on the practice of experienced teachers, on what they read and on the broad issues affecting schooling.

I think that this is a very helpful formulation and one that seems to fit closely with mentors' feelings about what students need as they develop over a year. However, I see the different types of reflection much more as strands than as levels. In the early parts of student teachers' experience they are almost desperate for the technical knowledge of 'getting it right' and then begin to see how evaluating the 'getting it right' leads to much greater skill and understanding – this is the practical kind of reflection; in simple terms, getting better. However, for example, they are aware that they are going through a rites of passage and a process that means that they are struggling with a new form of 'teacher self'. This 'teacher self' is made up of all kinds of selves, some of them representing societal and institutional limitations. Working through this struggle is one part of the more sophisticated kind of reflection. Inevitably this struggle only begins with student teaching and then takes many years to come to terms with. I believe, as does McIntyre, that student teachers need lots of help to get started on this process. I believe, even more firmly than he does, that student teachers need to work on all the levels concurrently and that skilled intervention helps them to sort out these different kinds of reflection and so to learn how to benefit from them. As I have argued above, student teachers can begin with concepts of the subject *in relation to their own experience*; this keeps the focus relevant and practical and does not make it feel distant from the student.

The mentor and reflective practice

A mentor combines two key roles at once. On the basis of the definition given above, that a reflective practitioner is someone who 'reflects systematically on her practice in a constant attempt to improve it', an English teacher who chooses to be a mentor is most likely to be a reflective practitioner and, I would argue, a good mentor must be one. A good mentor is someone for whom the idea of development is quintessential to her own work. Her desire to bring on others is a part of such a vision. That is the first role, that of the active and systematic supporter and developer of others.

The second role is that of the reflective practitioner who is always searching for that which is developmental. Working with a comparative novice is very demanding, especially when the expert is not content merely to show what she can do. That way of working tends to accentuate a kind of showmanship that may be pleasing to the expert's ego but is potentially damaging and limiting to the novice. The genuine reflective practitioner is always in learning mode, recognizing that in articulating their practice they are stimulating their own reflectiveness. Their dialogues with a student teacher will be real dialogues, especially as a student teacher in a reflective partnership will be able to ask the important questions that make both partners think hard about the topic in focus.

This model, once established, offers genuine opportunities for long-term development and, coupled with the notion of mentorship, provides a means by which mentor–comparative novice dialogues can be a consistent part of professional development. A good mentor, being a reflective practitioner, will employ that capability to develop others throughout their professional life. This point will be extended in Chapter 6.

The mentor, the student teacher and reflective practice

In the next chapter I will examine in great detail the multifarious role of the mentor, and so here I wish to conclude with a final emphasis on the crucial, underpinning principle of reflective practice. One of the great dangers of school-based teacher education is that it may become narrowed down to an apprenticeship model, or worse, to mere learning by imitation (see Chapter 1). If teachers in school, through constant demands on their time and energy, are given little time to reflect on their own practice and none to engage in serious dialogue with student teachers, then school-based teacher education will be a great step *backwards*. If there is to be a gain then resources should help to promote and support a reflective model. In the example I discussed, the mentor and students have time set aside each week to discuss each student's development. In every course evaluation I have undertaken, students stress how highly they value this time and how much difference it makes to them if the mentor gives it her full and thoughtful attention.

In such a model, and the dedicated time signals this, student teachers are already a valued part of the profession, not a nuisance to be tolerated. They are valued not only as people and as future teachers but as part of a *reflective profession*. Although much of their focus may be on the technical and practical elements of reflection, they are constantly prompting experienced teachers to reflect in the critical and emancipatory mode. In my own experience, English departments that I and my colleagues have rated as the best have always stressed that they value student teachers not for taking a few of their classes but for making them think and evaluate their practice. Here are a few indicative comments from mentors:

I really enjoy the dialogue with students – it has made me read a lot more 'theory' and helped me to think – their questions have often helped me to clarify my own views and reasons for doing things.

I believe that experienced practitioners have a genuine moral obligation to help new teachers, and anyway it has tremendous value for our professional development and the pupils.

It was a really good decision to get involved with the students and it has made me much more reflective about my own teaching – it has helped the whole department to think about the way we do things. Also the students bring such an influx of new ideas, it makes us think about new possibilities all the time – wonderful!

The students themselves really make you think but so do colleagues from other schools – meeting with them and university staff to talk about what student teachers of English need to know and experience has had a tremendously positive effect on me and my colleagues.

We have benefited from their ideas and enthusiasm and especially from having to make explicit our beliefs to genuinely interested but critical 'outsiders' – it is also so rewarding to feel that you are starting someone off on a good career.

So far we have looked closely at how significant a role the mentor has to play in helping the student teacher simply to think clearly about English. The more student teachers consider the subject the more they can help more experienced colleagues to reflect upon it and to clarify some of their own uncertainties and doubts. Whatever the uncertainties in other subject areas, there can be no doubt that English is one of the most politically and philosophically contentious, professionally controversial and personally opinionated areas of the curriculum; no wonder that students may want to push these matters aside in order to dive in at the deep end. Mentors can and, I would argue, should, articulate their beliefs and values about English, with the deliberate and conscious intention of making student teachers think through their own positions. Ultimately, of course, these beliefs and values matter most in the classroom, and it is time to look at how the mentor can help students in 'getting into the action'.

3 Becoming a mentor: managing the learning of student teachers of English

The role of the mentor: is it just like teaching?

So far we have looked closely at a number of the general challenges facing school-based teacher education and at some of the issues that tend to be particular to student teachers of English. In this chapter we shall examine in considerable depth the role of the mentor. As previously, some of the aspects of this chapter apply to any mentoring role, but some of the discussion, and certainly the examples, will focus on English teaching. Inevitably mentors themselves are all different and, within the general framework of the role, will find their own particular interpretation of how to make the most of it. In order to place mentoring in the appropriate context, we shall need first to examine some definitions about the purpose of teaching and about the nature of learning to teach. In seeking to become a reflective mentor as well as a reflective teacher, any teacher will recognize progressively that mentoring, like teaching, is always providing fresh challenges that stimulate learning. In other words, good mentors will continue to learn about mentoring as well as teaching.

It is worth repeating that mentoring is not like classroom teaching, and that many problems have been caused by simplistic assumptions that all teachers, being teachers, will automatically be able to teach novices to teach. I am not suggesting that this mistake has been made principally by teachers themselves. It is perhaps worth using the analogy with driving. All drivers have been 'taught' to drive and then usually drive a great deal for the rest of their lives. However, that does not make them necessarily expert, or even good, at driving, and it certainly does not make them good at passing on their driving skills to others, as many a seventeen year old will tell us. It is crucial to review from the beginning what a mentor's role can involve and to define this consistently in relation to classroom teaching to help keep differences, and some similarities, in the foreground.

The common goal: pupils' learning

If we start with the common goal, then this can be summed up, neatly and simply, as *learning for pupils*. In order for pupils to learn we try to create a particular kind of learning environment. For our purposes, we focus mainly on the classroom as the site where the most intensive learning for pupils may take place, but we obviously include the school as the larger context for the classroom and, rather paradoxically, society outside the school. Of course, these divisions are real physically but not real socially or culturally: the children live, as we do, in a messy reality where all kinds of factors are operating with and, frequently, against each other. However, it is worth stressing already that a mentor knows this point in a profound way that a student teacher, whatever her rhetoric, cannot know in the same way.

So, when we look at the goal of the student teacher, to become a good teacher in order to help pupils to learn, we see immediately that a mentor is facing a very new challenge. The effective teacher, in that special learning environment, makes a real difference to the learning of all the children. The mentor is likely to be such a teacher, but only one of many such teachers. The question is not 'How can this student teacher become like me?' but 'How can this student teacher learn to start becoming a good teacher?' The equation between the mentor and the mentee is very different from that between the teacher and a class, as, very obviously, the student teacher will not be taught to teach by the children, even though every class will certainly help that student teacher *to learn*. Just as a teacher is constantly looking for ways of improving the children's learning, so a mentor is constantly looking for ways of helping a student teacher to learn. The commonality here is in both planned and unplanned (but always principled) intervention. To put it simply and rather crudely, a group of children left alone together are likely to learn something, but we know that teachers' interventions, sometimes simply their presence, make a significant difference. A mentor is also looking to make that significant difference to the student teacher. In other words, left alone, particularly with a class, most student teachers will learn; what we are identifying at the outset is that the quality of such learning will be made significantly different, and much greater, through effective and skilful mentoring.

It is worth stressing how little time practising teachers have for learning from each other. Almost all the learning that goes on that involves colleagues might be called informal, even accidental, and takes place outside the classroom. There might seem to be an advantage here in that this might offer a model for the mentor–student teacher relationship. However, I think it fair to say that most teachers, for a host of reasons, become unconscious of this kind of learning. I also think it fair to say that much of this learning is on a relatively small scale; teachers are 'switching off' when they are 'free'. In-service courses tend to be, unsurprisingly, much more effective. Most of the time teachers are not consciously helping their colleagues to learn about teaching. Overall, then, most mentors have not been in many situations where their skills as teachers have been consciously redirected towards their colleagues. Part of the argument of this book is that we need to develop a profession where such activity becomes very normal and ordinary. Initially then, many mentors have to step back not only from their everyday teaching approach but also from the whole fabric of school life if they are to examine the mentor's role with a clear and unimpeded vision.

An interesting element in this requirement for the mentor to review practice is the increasing use of student teachers in pairs. Logistically this makes excellent sense, because a mentor can help both students to learn during, for example, the weekly tutorial. However, pairing students means that very different classroom learning situations can be organized. Instead of the 'traditional' model, in which the student observes the teacher until she 'takes over' the class, there are many more diverse and enriching opportunities and these will be discussed later in this chapter. The important point here is that most teachers have not themselves, either as student teachers or as regular teachers, experienced team teaching in any shape or form. Therefore, the opportunities presented to them by the possible use of an experienced teacher and two highly motivated novices in the same classroom do not fit with 'normal' practice. It is quite a different and novel situation, requiring a fresh approach aimed at bringing into harmony the learning of two adults and a group of children. The mentor is likely to orchestrate a learning environment in which the adults can learn, and this will require a very conscious level of attention to these adult learners. It is not that the children's experience need be very different from 'normal', except that it might be better, through more contact with, and attention from, interested adults.

Teaching as a highly skilled, complex activity

So what of the nature of teaching itself? I am certainly of the view that learning to teach is a highly complex activity in the way that teaching itself is always a highly complex activity. My own definition of teaching is that it is an intelligent and purposeful activity intended to promote learning, focused on and relating to the learners themselves, adopting the best means to achieve that end and engaging the motivation of the learners to maximize their learning. I appreciate that this sounds rather bitty, but I feel it teases out some of the key elements in teaching that get ignored in neater but more simplistic definitions. It immediately emphasizes that in finding a best means one teacher will, quite rightly, differ from another. There really is no one sure fire way to help children to enjoy poetry, but there is a great repository of ways of trying to help them, held in the professional knowledge of English teachers. A student teacher needs access to these 'ways' in order to select a 'best means' for any particular group of pupils.

I feel very strongly, then, that teaching is not merely a 'natural' activity, it is a learned and skilful one and it is vital for all mentors to review some ideas about how humans learn to be skilful. There is a long history of our investigations into how we came to be skilful (and also into why we still lack skill; take our motoring accident statistics, for example). This investigation began centuries ago, principally with philosophy; in the twentieth century most contributions have come from the younger field of psychology. I shall draw here on what I find valuable and the notes provide some further routes for interested readers.[1]

Almost all human action can be called skilled in the sense that it tends to be repeated and that under normal circumstances we reach a level of competence that allows us largely to forget that we are carrying it out. This is most obvious with predominantly physical actions, such as opening a door. There must be thousands of variants of handles and doors, yet most of the time I get through them without thinking literally about what I am doing; I am simply conscious of the wish or need to get to the other side.

However, there are much more complex activities that we generally recognize as such; few people will comment on your ability to open doors but they will perhaps notice how quickly or successfully you read or drive. Your awareness of these more complicated skills may have become equally habitual as opening doors; for example, for most of the time you are not at all aware of actually reading this page. The key point is that you are employing this skill with a reasoned purpose, you are (presumably) motivated to read. You have at your disposal a great many strategies of reading and, although reading is tiring, it is unlikely to require an enormous effort on your behalf; you have expertise as a reader. However, you may or may not be able to reproduce this page on a machine like a typewriter or word processor, depending on your skill as a typist and as a user of a particular kind of technology.

This latter skill is a useful one to help us think about learning teaching. To start with the obvious, someone can be highly skilled with language as a speaker, reader and writer (using a pen) but, apparently, utterly hopeless with a word processor. In fact, some existing knowledge will be a hindrance, because the infamous QWERTY keyboard bears little relation to the way English speakers tend to order things through alphabetization. Equally, the word processor's infinite capacity for change and correction is very dissimilar to the physical world of pen and paper.

Word processing is a highly skilled activity, drawing on a range of subskills, all of which can become, relatively, automatic. Writing with a word processor, as opposed to merely transposing someone else's writing, is even more skilled, bringing to bear far more of the intelligent purpose which informs teaching. Eventually, however, the analogy breaks down at the point of predictability. Writing and teaching are clearly very different types of highly skilled activity because, in contrast to word processing expertise, a teacher's expertise involves a constantly shifting set of variables with tendencies towards predictability but no absolute fixed outcomes.

Teaching is a highly complex situation and so tends to demand a kind of openness to complexity. In order to cope with this openness, teachers develop a great deal of what we all call know-how, what Schön calls 'knowledge-in-action' (Schön, 1983, 1987). Such know-how has become automatic and so is constantly, but not very *consciously*, available. A teacher does not consciously think 'What shall I do now?' Instead, through a constant monitoring of the situation, the teacher is employing a range of skills to maintain the learning of the pupils. Student teachers, of course, frequently think 'What shall I do now?' and, unfortunately, have no useful answer. This burying of know-how, below the conscious level, by an accomplished teacher, may frequently mean, as with driving, that she gets to the end of the lesson/journey with little recall of the skilled actions she took. In fact, in order to cope with the one or two hazardous and challenging moments of the lesson/journey, which she does remember, it is important that the other routine aspects are 'forgotten'. We might describe this apparent paradox as the employment of relatively closed skills which are rarely conscious (when you apply the brakes the car slows down) and open skills where the mind is, however briefly, consciously engaged (if I brake sharply now the car behind will hit us but I need to slow down enough to avoid the car which is turning left). The latter, open skill, is always monitoring the range of complexity, recognizing, of course, that however expert we are we may still make a mistake if we do not pay attention. The passenger in the car, who does not read the road like a driver (like the student teacher who does not 'read' the class), is likely to have no idea that there was any danger or that the problem was skilfully solved.

To sum up, any skilled activity becomes increasingly unconscious and more intuitive. An aspect of this intuitiveness is that humans tend to develop patterns of action, sometimes called 'chunks'; these are fairly fixed routines of behaviour that have become associated with gaining successful outcomes. This is especially important for mentors to recognize, as it means that whole sequences of skilful teaching may seem to them like one action; to a student teacher they are invisible and, as a sequence, impossible to imitate. I used an example earlier in the text where Joyce taught a smoothly sequenced poetry lesson that Angela, the student teacher, could only appreciate at the pupil level. She could not 'see the joins' in the sequence, and neither, of course, could Joyce. A mentor has to learn how to break down these chunks into pieces suitable for a novice to recognize and then assimilate. Another key point about skilled behaviour is that it will at times work at a very conscious level, especially when the expertise is not producing the desired outcomes. Hence we say things like 'That has really got me thinking' or 'I just can't explain that,' and we are then drawing, fully and consciously, on our entire repertoire of knowledge.

A very salutary point for mentors is that there is no necessary correlation between expertise and either the analysis of, or the communication of, that expertise. In fact, one of the paradoxes of highly skilled activity is that it may well become increasingly difficult to articulate, except to an absolute peer, an equivalent expert. 'Expert' has become a tricky term in recent years and I would feel very confident that most teachers would never use such a term about themselves or their colleagues. Personally, I think this is unfortunate, and part of a historical syndrome through which teachers have played their knowledge, and their expertise, down so low that they have trouble recognizing it themselves. Putting the problems with the term 'expert' aside, the key point is that experts, in any field, use what is pejoratively called jargon and what might be positively, and more sensibly, referred to as professional terminology. Whatever this language is called, it is especially incomprehensible to the outsider and particularly challenging to the novice, to whom it may appear deliberately exclusive. Mentors are, once more, in a very challenging role as mediators of this language, but they must also face up to the strange notion that they are made, potentially at least, inarticulate by their expertise. All mentors will need to consider, as they always do with children, how to get a particular point 'across' to a novice whose grasp of the descriptive language of teaching is as limited as her understanding.

Finally, once we achieve a high level of skill, we certainly can go on learning, i.e. getting better, and some of this learning may actually be at a mainly unconscious level; we are no longer conscious that we are learning and certainly feel no effort involved. However, it is also likely, and not a contradiction, that we may reach a level of competence that means that we are on a kind of plateau. This is where it is important to emphasize that the model of the reflective practitioner is not necessarily the same as that of the effective teacher. The effective teacher may still be learning in a rather incidental and effortless way, and so still improving, but the reflective practitioner is consciously and systematically trying to improve, and this clearly requires considerable effort. It is also the kind of conscious effort that a mentor needs to make to help a student teacher to learn about teaching.

Learning to teach

Given that teaching is so complex, how can it be 'learnt'? In the first two chapters I have discussed a diverse range of ways in which the process of learning about teaching may be begun and then, steadily, built upon. However, it is important now to break down the main cycle that mentors have to deal with in school. This stage may, put crudely, be called 'learning by doing', and inevitably this is how it is usually perceived by students. This stage, however dominated by the idea of 'doing', is far more complex than this simplistic description suggests, and a mentor has a very sophisticated role to play in making it a successful stage for student teachers.

The simplest and very familiar formulation of the teaching cycle is:

- planning;
- teaching;
- evaluating.

This is a kind of endless loop. I would want to argue for more detail here, especially if a mentor is going to make that significant difference that the role is intended to and that we have begun to explore. The planning stage incorporates what the student teacher already knows about teaching. It is therefore also a time of reflection and then selection from a range of possibilities, some observed, some tried and some, perhaps, simply read about or described by others. Student teachers, as we all know, find planning extremely time-consuming and difficult, even writing down an actual script, word by word, for each lesson. Essentially, the planning needs to become increasingly their own, but initially a mentor has much guidance to offer. A plan is simply a representation of what 'should happen' in order to achieve the desired learning outcomes, and experienced teachers treat it as a sketch and not the full picture. A student teacher wants a blueprint that is immaculate, leaving no room for error. As one student once expressed it to me, 'The teachers approve all my plans and then I find out when I am teaching that they are full of mistakes!' The mentor is a key figure in helping the student teacher to have both the security implicit in the blueprint and the artistry and interpretation left open by the sketch. Readers will sense, or know already, that this is one of the most challenging aspects of the role.

For student teachers the unit of teaching may begin as a few minutes, moving up to significant proportions of a lesson, on to whole lessons and so on. For them it seems especially important to formulate this as what Tomlinson, in the excellent *Understanding Mentoring*, calls the 'teaching attempt' (Tomlinson, 1994: 17). This stresses the idea that it is properly a trial and error session, a trying out of the earlier planning attempt. What highly skilled teachers do, during their teaching, is what Schön calls 'reflection-in-action'. They are constantly evaluating and monitoring the learning environment, making reasoned adjustments and alterations, even making major changes to their original expectations, all without apparent effort or loss of momentum. Such reflection-in-action is entirely invisible to all but the most skilled observer and would require a special kind of effort for the teacher to articulate afterwards. Student and beginning teachers are rarely able to achieve this reflection-in-action, so almost all of their reflection will be done *outside the classroom*. Not surprisingly, much of their reflection is, to put it rather negatively, as inexpert as their teaching (see Chapter 2). They can achieve, especially with skilled help, *reflection-on-action*, and this seems to help to move them towards less dependence on the planned script and on the advice of others.

When evaluating the teaching attempt, student teachers are especially prone to confusion. Sorting out what happened in the classroom is highly problematic and, although careful observation of other teachers can help them considerably (see chapter 4), they are very unskilled at reading the classroom. As I will argue later, student teachers are highly vulnerable, especially in their first attempts at evaluation, and benefit very little from having 'what went wrong' pointed out to them. Not surprisingly, experienced observers, applying their own criteria, will generally have seen far more 'going wrong' than the novice. The student thinks that she 'did what you said', the teacher emphatically states the opposite and all we have is a gulf. The mentor, I would argue, must be capable of reflection-in-action, not now as a teacher, but *as a mentor*. The mentor may already have helped with the planning and teaching of a lesson, but will need to be just as active in its evaluation, though not as a simplistically judgemental figure. In order to pinpoint where advice and dialogue may be productive, a mentor will need to be understanding of the student teacher's account of the lesson. Once more the formulation might be better expressed as an attempted evaluation, which a mentor figure helps to improve. As the evaluation progresses, or as the student and mentor discuss the student's existing evaluation, so the mentor needs to be responsive, as with a class, to the needs and confusions of the student.

Even for the most expert teacher teaching is a tiring and frequently frustrating business; for the student teacher these elements may be multiplied many times over. A mentor has to maintain a student teacher's motivation as much as her emergent expertise. If you are trying to become skilled then coaching and advice can make a tremendous difference not only to 'how' you try it next time but also to whether you believe it is worth trying at all. An attempted evaluation can become a successful one if the outcome is positive and coherent; a student teacher is unlikely to achieve these outcomes without skilful intervention and support.

Phases of learning to teach

Psychological research and educational research[2] have tended to agree on the phases that student teachers tend to pass through on their way to becoming competent, and I feel sure that readers will feel familiar with these from their own experience. The first phase is usually termed *cognitive*; that is, when the student is trying to get clear about what to do. At this stage they tend to hold a simplistic view of successful teaching and often just wish to be told what to do in order to do 'it' properly. This phase corresponds with what might be called *unconscious incompetence*; that is, the student is unaware that she cannot do what the experienced teacher is doing.

The second phase brings much greater awareness, and repeated attempts at just doing it properly problematize the whole concept of successful teaching. Initially, this includes some *conscious incompetence*; that is, a recognition of how hard teaching is to get right. Overall, this is the *associative* phase, where student teachers begin to make sense of the different forms of advice they have received and consciously to incorporate these various elements into their own teaching, achieving some *conscious competence* as a result.

The third phase can be described as the *intuitive* phase, where some things are becoming automatic and unconscious and so the teaching is much more economical in terms of effort and concentration. This improvement frees up a good deal of mental space for faster learning of even more skilful teaching. In that sense the student has broken through into a new phase that literally feels qualitatively different. This is not only conscious competence but the beginning of a potentially far more powerful reflective cycle in which the beginning teacher has enough stability in her teaching to focus on selected elements. There is a parallel here even with knowledge of a class; once a student teacher begins to use, publicly, the names of all the children in a class, and not just those of children who are 'difficult', I usually feel that this is a sign of a fairly stable situation.

I think it also important to emphasize here that once a student is consciously competent she is able to learn more; she has not reached a plateau. It might be tempting at the point where the student teacher is 'doing fine now' to, in a sense, leave her alone, the job being done. However, school-based teacher education means that the mentor has a powerful role right up until students finish their course. What may be at issue is the mentor's judgement of where, along a kind of continuum of competence, a particular student has reached.

The phases of learning to teach and the mentor's interventions

I hope that my analysis of the learning to teach cycle fits reasonably well with the reader's own. I am not, however, claiming that I am offering an exact description, simply a useful formulation that should help a skilful mentor to think about how to make a significant difference to a student teacher's learning. Mentoring is a multi-purpose role and, in the course of the book, a number of these roles will be examined. In this section I want to concentrate on the concept of the intervention, providing more concrete examples in Chapter 4. The next chapter will also look closely at the very personal nature of mentoring. Many functions of the mentor are similar to those of the counsellor. I am not leaving out the human dimension from this next section but for purposes of clarity I am going to begin by examining learning about teaching and how thoughtful interventions can be productive of that learning, looking later at the inevitably problematic nature of human interactions under stressful conditions.

I feel that mentors have a general sequence to bear in mind when planning their overall strategy with student teachers:

- reviewing;
- planning;

- action;
- monitoring;
- feedback.

These terms can be kept in mind whatever the action 'in the middle' may be. Much of the time the action is teaching or a closely linked kind of activity, but it might equally be observation, attending a parent's evening or planning an interview with the special educational needs coordinator.

I am using the term *reviewing* to stress the need to be constantly taking stock. First we have the very important issue of preconceptions. I have discussed aspects of this issue in Chapter 1, but it is certainly worth focusing on the point again from a rather different angle. Reviewing points up the need for both partners, student and mentor, to talk about what they already know and what they expect to be happening later on. In literal terms this element may not be separate from planning, but I believe it is a crucial emphasis. As an example, a mentor and student are planning some observation of the mentor's own teaching. The mentor might say, 'I will probably put them in groups for a few minutes.' To the student, especially early on, this may sound like a straightforward action; however, almost certainly, the mentor may, quite unintentionally, mislead the student here. 'Putting children into groups' is usually an apparently simple action but is, in fact, a highly complex element in all teaching, and, I would argue, especially in English teaching, it is one of the 'chunks' in teaching described above. It contains a meta-level, partly about the value of group work in learning, partly about the particular role of group work in English. It then contains a number of sub-levels to do with the composition of groups (ability, gender, personality etc.), the history of group work in that class and so on. At different stages, student teachers will have more of a grasp of what 'putting them in groups' can actually mean; in early discussions of this 'action', there will be considerable need for mentors to explain and/or discuss, even quite painstakingly, what is involved and what the point of this apparently simple action might be.

It is inevitable that a mentor will not have the time to discuss every detail of all lessons because they are, typically, highly complex interactions. It is also important for the mentor to use a strategy that she will frequently employ with children; that is, identifying how far and how fast to go with something new. A skilful mentor will recognize how different student teachers, like children, have different capacities for learning, but early on, especially, student teachers are quickly overloaded. So, if the group work is actually a key part of the lesson the mentor will have to point this out and consider how to help the student teacher to observe this so that something may be observed and discussed later.

Part of the discussion about planning will include some form of review of 'group work'. The mentor will need to stand back from her practice, take the automatic element 'off' her planning and actually articulate its purpose. She will also need to bring to the surface the student's own preconceptions and value judgements about the purpose and function of groups, particularly in the context of English. Perhaps this all sounds very obvious but in practice it is not so. In order for a student teacher to learn from observing teaching, a mentor will have to intervene in a productive way and this concept of reviewing should help both parties.

Planning should incorporate this review process, and then student and mentor can focus on being clear about the purpose and aims of the activity, its context and what the choices are for strategies and approach. Expert practitioners do not 'appear' to plan consciously and we are once more requiring the mentor to review her own practice. Not only do accomplished teachers appear not to plan but they can, as with the poetry lesson example in Chapter 2, downplay the idea of planning. By seeming not to need to plan they may confuse students about their (the students') need to plan extensively and in detail. Unfortunately, some teachers are even disparaging about lesson plans and evaluations. 'You only have to do that to please the college tutors' is a comment that student teachers frequently recount. To me these are not simply unprofessional remarks, they are also completely wrong. Student teachers need to plan because they do not know what to do. Accomplished teachers do know what to do, so they already have a plan; a mentor needs to identify where the students are and to engage with their plans. Over the course of time the student will take more and more responsibility for planning but a mentor can always help with the process. Initially the student must be able to understand plans, whoever is producing them. Finally, it is a myth that experienced teachers do not plan. They tend not to plan consciously when they are using very familiar material in familiar contexts. However, whenever these variables change they certainly do plan and, because they are in fact highly skilled at planning, they are able to plan very effectively. The reflective practitioner, I would argue, continues to plan at both the level of the lesson and the level of the whole teaching cycle of a particular group; for example, two years for a GCSE group. Student teachers have a particular need to have planning 'taught' to them, and not just by sessions 'at college'.

During the *action* stage, the student teacher will have a very limited ability to monitor what is happening. This is just as true of initial observation, when the student is apparently 'just sitting there taking notes'. A mentor will be monitoring not only her teaching and the class, but also the student. In other words, a mentor is usually a better judge of the student teacher's role as observer than the student, as well as of the class and the teaching itself. *Monitoring* while teaching is one of the most demanding of all skills and also one of the least observable by others. It corresponds with the intuitive nature of expert teaching discussed above. A good teacher is monitoring without being conscious of the activity, as it were, reading the classroom like a page. The student teacher, however, is learning to 'read'.

So when the *feedback* stage comes there is a great deal to do to establish what the action was in relation to the original plan and the actual outcome. A student teacher cannot feedback consciously to an experienced teacher in a way that interacts easily with the experienced teacher's needs. We must deal with the student teacher's needs. A mentor may well need to start by simply asking 'What did you see?' and should not be surprised that it was a different lesson from the one the mentor may have taught. This is not a real problem, it is simply an example of the way we all construct what we see. Differences of perception are normal and should be accepted as such. Many a mentor has commented to me on how the naiveté of a student teacher's questions has first taken her breath away but then made her reflect very powerfully on an important aspect of teaching.

The mentor's feedback is one of the most powerful sources of learning about teaching that the student teacher will have. It immediately enters into the review and planning stages, helping the student to put everything into some kind of meaningful perspective, often turning apparently negative experiences into positive learning points. This sequence – *review, planning, action, monitoring and feedback* – provides a basic approach to many mentoring functions. Frequently, these elements are overlapping and, for a student teacher to become more competent, she must be able to make them overlap. It is helpful, then, if a mentor is explicit in what she is doing and actually uses terminology like 'Let us review what we have agreed about group work.' Such explicitness may sound over-formal, but it actually helps student teachers a great deal and certainly helps the mentor to be conscious of what she is doing, so following the model of the reflective practitioner.

Making the most of student teachers' learning

A mentor, as mentioned already, several times, fulfils a number of roles. One role might be described as *orchestrating*; that is, organizing a series of experiences and contexts for student teachers, in order to provide them with powerful, but also protected, learning opportunities. We have already considered the learning cycle of students, the five element intervention (review, plan, action, monitor and feedback), the danger of overloading them and the demands on the mentors to stand back from and to articulate their practice. Now we need to consider the sources of learning that mentors can provide for students.

Currently most student teachers joining a course, as described in Chapter 1, have undertaken a reasonable amount of preparation. Such preparation is undoubtedly useful, but it is only a beginning and should be viewed as such. This preparation may have already included some observation, but 'some observation' is not the same as really focused observation assisted by a skilled mentor or tutor. Mentors can rightly expect student teachers to come to their school well informed and receptive to their help, but any more is likely to be unrealistic.

Inevitably, and appropriately, the first source of learning in school is going to be observation. However, it is most important to stress that this source of learning is much enhanced by a broad awareness of issues; I shall focus on this below. A mentor has many choices when she comes to consider some kind of systematic programme of observation for student teachers. A simple and somewhat 'traditional' model involves simply putting students in as many different rooms with as many different teachers as possible in an intense period. This has the virtue of offering the student a total immersion in school life; however, there is some danger of drowning in such an approach. I would argue that student teachers do not learn very much from such an approach, but they certainly feel that they have undergone some kind of rites of passage, and one thing should not be mistaken for the other. Student teachers may actually end up with the impression that they have, somehow, 'arrived', have done their necessary observation and can now 'get on' with the real job. So such a stage is useful, but more in its general orientation than for what a student teacher learns about skilful teaching; such knowledge comes later and very gradually.

Most courses ask mentors to balance subject focus with whole-school focus, and this demands that students do not exclusively spend their time in the English classroom. However, subject mentors are *subject* mentors and they, like their student teachers, can tend to feel that the specialism is everything. I would suggest that a good mentor will recognize two crucial points here. First, good observation, is properly *selective*, and, second, a student's understanding is very considerably enhanced by her being helped to put the English classroom in the context of *the whole school* and of the total experience of individual pupils. One test of the quality of a good school-based course, certainly in my opinion, is whether students are given a broad view of school life. Such a view would include:

- a planned induction to the whole school;
- a planned programme of discussions about whole-school topics that relates closely to the elements of the HE programme;
- access to whole school policies, Ofsted reports etc.;
- briefing about links with external agencies such as social workers and collaborative ventures such as links with industry;
- a range of opportunities to work within the pastoral system (including direct experience of form tutoring);
- the teaching of personal and social education (or its equivalent);
- opportunities for involvement in whole-school events like training days, parents' evenings and trips;
- joining in differing types of extra-curricular activity.

I would also argue for students undertaking a whole-school assignment of some kind. In my experience such assignments have been not only very developmental for the student but of considerable use to the school. Generally these topics are negotiated between the student, the school and the HEI, allowing the student and, potentially, the school to benefit from a serious review of a

key school issue. Very occasionally student teachers' research uncovers problems that some members of staff would rather were left covered up. Such
controversial work is rare but when it happens it is obviously a source of
tension and requires some delicate diplomacy to be employed. Mentors, knowing
their mentees very well, may find themselves with a helpful role to play in
such circumstances; this will be further discussed in Chapter 4.

The list of whole-school activities above is certainly long, but it is a distinct
advantage of school-based teacher education that student teachers are in school
long enough to benefit from such a programme and to be able to contribute
valuably to it. Overall then, I am stressing that this whole-school approach is
significant for a student teacher's experience; it should be a part of the planned
cycle of her learning and should add a very proper balance to her subject
specialism. I think it important that subject mentors are not only clear about
what students are doing on 'that side' of the course, but that they actively
encourage students to be balanced. Almost all secondary classroom teachers
define themselves by their subject ('I am a teacher of X'), and student teachers
are really quite desperate to become a specialist. A subject mentor, perhaps
rather ironically, is in a key position to influence the student away from such
a narrow perception of the job of a teacher.

Over the course of the year, coordination between these two sides is really
important; we have noted the danger of overload for student teachers, but
must also recognize that there can be what I sometimes call *subject-selfishness*.
This phenomenon comes, as usual, from the very best intentions and from the
pressures of 'real life'. A subject teacher can feel very strongly that what a
student teacher needs is as much time in the English classroom as possible.
However, I am arguing that a mentor, however passionate and enthusiastic
about the subject, has a broader responsibility and must, at times, resist this
'subject-selfishness' for the long-term benefit of the student and, ultimately, of
the children she will work with. Such resistance cannot be merely passive to
be effective: subject mentors often need to steer their mentees towards whole-
school concerns.

To return to the place of observation but briefly to continue this point,
when a student is first in school and raring to get into the English classroom
she also benefits enormously from regaining some perspective on the child's
experience of the highly fragmented, secondary curriculum. A common, and
excellent, practice is for student teachers to shadow a class, or even an individual pupil, for a whole day or longer, systematically recording what happens
in different lessons. An English student teacher can be encouraged to make
special notes on the way the four language modes are employed in different
lessons.

Most secondary courses include some time in primary school, again an
excellent practice. Student teachers must actually demonstrate knowledge of
the position of their subject within the primary curriculum, with particular
attention to transition from Key Stages 2 to 3. However, there is a real need to

put the subject into a perspective that recognizes its place within the whole curriculum at primary and secondary levels. Once again, student teachers are expected to understand how their subject contributes to the curriculum in relation to other subjects, but the students themselves need real help with maintaining at times a whole-school and, therefore, pupil-centred view of school life. Finally, such whole-school observation techniques usually feature early on in a student teacher's experiences, but there is a very strong case for them to return to such approaches later in their course, once both their observational skills and their general awareness have improved. As always, the subject mentor has an important role to play in directing a student teacher towards a balanced experience throughout the course.

Most students will receive considerable help with observation techniques as part of their HE course. Some courses have negotiated agreed approaches, including detailed checklists, with their partnership schools. Some schools have taken great care to design their own observation formats. Mentors will need to be informed about these points in order to build on previous work and to complement it. Clearly their information should partly be supplied by the HEI and/or the school, but, as with other issues, a mentor can very usefully begin, with the student, with the review stage: 'What do we know about observing, what are we trying to achieve?' Student teachers may immediately react to this by saying something like, 'My tutor says we have to do so and so.' The likelihood, in my experience, is that this is an exaggeration of what the tutor said and that the mentor, having agreed the programme with the tutor anyway, will know that it is. So the mentor will want, and need, to direct the student, or students, to manageable observational tasks. It is impossible here to offer the huge list of possible tasks, so we can focus on some indicative examples and how they may be sequenced to enhance student teacher learning.

Student teachers may be characterized, by tutors and mentors, as unskilled observers, seeking to become skilled. However, that may not be their own categorization. As stressed in Chapter 1, student teachers have so much 'experience' of school that they believe that they know, rightly in one sense, a great deal, and they also have strong views about English teaching. However, a good deal of this 'knowledge' will simply interfere with the new, teacherly perspective that they need to develop. A mentor's important, initial task is to help a student teacher to recognize her *lack* of observation skill, but without lessening her motivation or her ability to recognize the value of selective observation. This can only really happen through discussion of observation, not simply through the observation itself; being an unskilled observer, a student teacher genuinely does not know 'what to look for'. The analogy with driving is once more useful: sitting in a car for thousands of hours simply provides a familiarity with driving that is extraordinarily unlike the experience of driving oneself.

Students need motivation to observe well, as otherwise observation is not simply unproductive, it may actually be demotivating and confirm student teachers' misjudgements; for example, that good teaching looks easy and so is easy. Equally, becoming consciously incompetent as an observer is an unsettling and potentially demotivating process. Learning to read the classroom is extremely challenging and frequently mentors themselves have had very little experience of either observing or being observed. Changes in schools, such as appraisal, more frequent inspections and school-based teacher education, mean that observing is becoming more common. However, observation is a skill that takes time and practice to acquire. Mentors may well need a good deal of practice in order to be effective as both observers and directors of student observation. I offer a suggestion about this in the next section of the chapter. To return to student teachers' 'conscious incompetence', they will benefit from feeling that observation is not only valuable but given high status by the mentor who acknowledges its difficulty and who engages the student in discussing the purpose of any observational task, often providing the student with a choice, a choice carefully limited by the mentor to help the student to make a sensible and manageable decision, which still makes her feel some personal investment in the choice made.

Once a mentor is prepared and wants to begin a programme of observation for a student, a useful process might be outlined as follows, and I recognize its ideal nature, but I know many good mentors and this is certainly how they tend to operate. The mentor begins by identifying what is possible in the short term, say the next few lessons, possibly a week or so (later on it may be feasible to plan for much larger chunks of time). Then the tasks are discussed and the student is guided about the implications of such tasks, then an agreement is reached about how the student will select from the observations what is most important and then a time is identified for the mentor–student discussion.

In the early stages of the course, the mentor is likely to want to move the student forward 'on all fronts', so, for example, there may be some lessons in which the content itself is especially important for observation. Normally a mentor will know that the HEI is looking at, say, poetry teaching that week (because the mentor will have the published programme), and so can offer a student teacher a chance to look at some poetry teaching in the department. Or perhaps the HEI focus is on fiction reading and, as well as offering some observation opportunities, the mentor suggests that the student interviews her year 7 class in small groups to discuss their interests and habits as readers. The mentor may guide the student for an agreed proportion of the day, say two lessons, to focus solely on teacher–pupil interactions: 'What do teachers say, what do pupils say?' There might even be an observational emphasis solely on questions. The mentor might suggest that the student looks closely at 'management': how is the lesson started and finished; how does the teacher make things happen; how long do sections of the lesson last; does the teacher say afterwards that the lesson went according to plan or were there changes? The student, as mentioned above, is then expected to report back to the mentor and *to select* some key points for discussion. In this approach the student must reflect first on what, given the strict limits of both time and her capacity to absorb ideas, is worth discussing in some depth. This approach should help the student teacher to acquire the habit of reflection and to respect the time limits that make such reflection, and selection of focus, so crucial.

Early on in the course the mentor will also need to be directive, with some negotiation, to engage the student's motivation. As the student develops observation skills, so the mentor can negotiate far more of the observational content, always encouraging the student to review and reflect on previous observation, so building up an understanding of where the student has 'got to'. It is extremely likely that the student will observe the mentor's teaching. This relationship can be highly productive of the student teacher's learning, but, on occasion, difficult and even upsetting, and the mentor has to be prepared for such trying moments; this will be discussed further in Chapter 4. Concentrating on the positive outcomes for now, by using her own classes the mentor can actually provide the extra dimension that is usually missing from most observation. In most observational situations the student only gets to have concerns clarified after the lesson is over; of course, because of teaching demands sometimes these concerns are never even discussed. Using her own classes, a skilful mentor can help the student understand the monitoring that is going on, even as the lesson progresses; later this role can be reversed so that the student teacher can seek either advice or guidance as her lesson progresses, or does not, as the case may be. In this sense a student can really ask, 'What should I do now?' and there will be a skilled teacher there to say, 'Well, you could try this or this.' Clearly this benefits the student teacher but it also, very importantly, benefits the class. Initially, the student teacher is least aware of monitoring, and therefore can gain immensely from brief conversations with the mentor, who can be explaining how and why her lesson is progressing as it is. It must be stressed that the monitoring process is the most intuitive part of teaching and it is likely that a mentor may have to keep reminding herself to explain to a student what seems blindingly obvious and in no need of explanation.

Getting into the action

For the student teacher, the mentor and the HE tutor, the whole point of all the careful orchestration of preparation and observation is that the student will have a successful teaching experience. School-based teacher education provides an ideal opportunity to move on from some rather tired arguments about how student teachers should have their baptism of fire to a more enlightened and more thoughtful approach. There is a simplistic concept, still prevalent among some people, that teachers are basically born, so if you throw one into a proverbial deep end, the 'true' teacher will float. This seems rather like the medieval approach to witches but in reverse: if they floated they were guilty and so drowned and if they drowned they were not witches – just dead. This old concept is equally odd, because people tend not to say 'Brain surgeons are born not made' or 'You can't teach airline pilots, they can either fly jumbo jets or they cannot.' I confess that I am labouring the point, but I do firmly believe, as I have mentioned earlier on, that whenever teachers utter these comments about teachers being 'naturals', they undermine and belittle the whole profession. I am not in the slightest bit concerned here to elevate teacher educators, although they could certainly do with far more professional support too, but I am concerned to help mentors resist this outdated notion. This is not to say that 'learning by doing' is a poor way to learn; it is, on the contrary, highly productive. We simply do not put learner drivers in the fast lane of the motorway during their first lesson, however keen they might be to 'have a go'.

The key point is that the mentor has a crucial role to play in managing the student teacher's gradual introduction to whole-class teaching. Most partnership courses are very clear in their documentation about ways that student teachers can move from observation to whole-class teaching, and this section should simply help mentors to identify their role in the process. The longer period in school takes some of the pressure off the first attempts at teaching and gives mentors and students more opportunities to focus on ensuring reasonably successful 'teaching attempts'.

It is simplest to identify two major phases: first, *progressively collaborative teaching*, followed by *increasingly independent teaching*. In the first phase, the mentor can involve the student in a planned progression. Students, when observing, are often invited to 'wander round and muck in'. This is often a surprisingly tough step. However, in one sense, it is what students need to do: I would just suggest that there are more focused and productive ways to help them 'muck in' that will be more helpful in their initial professional development. A simple point is that if a student is to make progress, understand that progress and have a sense of development, then classroom tasks need to be identified that can be evaluated. 'Mucking in' is vague and awkward, and brings the student into contact with the children in the most random way. However, if the mentor says something as simple as, 'During this writing activity, I am going to help this half of the room and Miss A will help the other half,' then everyone is clear and the children have already to treat Miss A as equal. Mentors will no doubt think of their own first steps for student teachers, but quite subject-specific contributions like reading poetry or a story aloud to a class, writing instructions on the board and talking the class through them, leading a brief discussion and so on are excellent beginnings. Equally, they might be more management-focused, taking responsibility for a transition during a lesson, giving out homework at the end of a lesson, preparing a worksheet and checking that pupils are clear about how to use it. These subject/management distinctions are rather artificial, but they do help students to focus and deal with lesson segments in a distinct and meaningful way and then to discuss them in a manageable framework.

As the student develops, so the mentor and student can jointly plan a lesson, identifying 'who does what' and gradually increasing the responsibility of the student to make the key decisions, before and during the lesson. This approach clearly involves 'learning by doing', but always within a reasonably manageable context. The doing element is constantly interspersed with opportunities for discussion and reflection. The systematic focus on elements of teaching allows the mentor and student to concentrate on these elements. As with other kinds of skill acquisition, particular sub-skills are best practised when they are understood in relation to the whole process, but isolating them makes both the skill and the process more meaningful, especially when an expert is able to put both the part and the whole in perspective. We are looking at how what I called earlier 'the teaching attempt' can be a constant source of genuine experiment, but in usefully controlled conditions.

Student teachers are always working towards the basic goal of independent teaching. Moving from phase 1, progressively collaborative teaching, to phase 2, increasingly independent teaching, should be relatively smooth in school-based teacher education. All partnership courses have at least one, and often two, periods of 'main practice' when the student will be taking responsibility for several classes. In some courses the student will already have worked for a considerable length of time with some classes, building up a relationship, before 'taking over'. It is possible to arrange this transition so that the pupils are practically unaware that their 'regular' teacher has now become the observer or classroom helper.

Overall, however the transition is managed, student teachers will need plenty of time to be 'alone with a class'. I will discuss in the next chapter some issues about status and authority in the classroom, but at this point it is worth stressing that a mentor can continue to give plenty of support in, and out of, the classroom, as the student becomes increasingly independent. The transition does mean, however, some 'letting go' by the mentor. It is inevitable that classes miss their highly skilled teacher when she is replaced by someone who is far less competent, although children are resiliently fickle about who they 'miss' and seem quite happy to switch 'loyalties' on a daily basis. More seriously, a mentor needs to think through, in relation to the individual student teacher, how to withdraw from the situation in order to give the student teacher the maximum opportunity to learn about teaching. Given that good mentors will inevitably try to provide a valuable range of classes for students to work with, there is no need for 'independent teaching' to mean the same with each group. Students need exposure to the full range of challenges in school, but they do not need to experience the sometimes crushing weight of total responsibility for all those challenges, and, for example, student and mentor might work collaboratively with a difficult group right through the year to the mutual benefit of everyone concerned. A mentor might well work with a pair of student teachers in one class, throughout the time they are in school, in order to give certain children really special attention and the students a chance to gain special insights. Student teachers themselves can gain an immense amount from becoming very knowledgeable about individual children. Often getting to know children can take years, as beginning teachers struggle to manage five or six classes a day. Students can gain powerful insights into learning through such carefully organized experiences. These experiences may not look like the 'real thing', and some teachers have expressed worries that student teachers will not be able to cope with the real thing later and that they had better get used to the harsh realities right now. Again, I think this is well intentioned but not particularly helpful. What we all want is teachers who can help children to learn and who are learning themselves; we want teachers who can indeed deal with the realities of school life but in a positive and confident way.

Finally, in order to become useful to a student teacher's long-term development, the mentor will need to begin to stand back from the classrooms with which she is intensely familiar. As will be discussed in the next chapter, the mentor–mentee relationship is always important, frequently intense and often fraught. A mentor will have to make sound, professional judgements about a student teacher's competence based on clear and systematically gathered evidence. The bottom line is that a student's future career (in teaching or somewhere else) rests in the hands of a mentor (see Chapter 5).

I would argue that good partnership courses are much more balanced than this implies, and they neither leave a mentor in such a singular position nor leave any individual involved in crucial professional judgements in such an onerous one. In a good partnership, judgements will be reached through open negotiation between the mentor, who is also representing her colleagues, the HEI tutor and the student. In difficult cases, others will be involved. Most HEIs have an external examiner system and most schools have a senior member of staff in charge of all students. Such figures can be invaluable when assessment has become complicated or difficult through unusual circumstances.

To return to the basic point, a mentor is partial, probably close to the student teacher in some ways and close to many children involved, but equally seeking to be impartial, in order to reach fair and reasonably objective judgements. So a mentor partly has to let go of teaching classes to become more of an observer and more, when appropriate, of an evaluator. The process of evaluating the student teacher's work will be discussed in great depth in Chapter 4.

Preparation and resources for mentoring

I hope I have made a strong case, so far, for the demanding nature of skilful mentoring. Mentoring places considerable demands on the resourcefulness of the individual, her department and her institution. School-based teacher education should, in my view, with the right balance of elements, produce effective and thoughtful English teachers. However, as discussed in Chapter 2, it requires more resources than the 'old' system to make it work and it is more prone to inequalities of provision for the student teacher. There is no way of avoiding the fact that a mentor is being given a very real responsibility and no one should undertake the role lightly.

Mentoring, as discussed above, is different enough from the classroom teaching of children to require a very considerable change of approach. Many of the points made above should enable a current mentor to review her practice to see how it is developing and to think ahead about planned change, where needed.

As with learning to teach, a broad knowledge is extremely valuable. Understanding how teacher education has operated in the past, and why it now operates in the way that it does, are elements included in this book precisely because mentors need a broad and comprehensive understanding of the actual and possible contexts for school-based teacher education. For most mentors, background reading will be a powerful aid to reflective practice, and I offer some suggestions in the notes.

Learning from colleagues in a formal and informal way may be equally important. Any school which has several departments involved should bring subject mentors together to discuss common issues and objectives and to review each year's work. Mentors change, and this process can also be planned, when possible, so that next year's mentor shadows this year's, providing a relatively smooth and problem-free transition. Most HEIs provide opportunities for subject mentors to meet, and an increasing number are offering qualifications to help give mentorship both the right level of training and the high status that it deserves.

Ultimately, resources are a key issue, and in my course example in Chapter 2, I described how one course provides two full-day meetings a year for subject mentors and approximately one hour per week to meet a pair of students. Everyone involved recognizes that this is nothing like enough time and that mentors, as well as many other teachers, give enormous amounts of their time to support and advise students. However, the designated time is just that, time given for the specific purpose of mentoring student teachers; it is protected time and therefore at least has the right status. Student teachers themselves rate this time, alongside visits from HEI tutors, as one of the most important elements in their whole year's experience; they never underrate its importance.

Schools that are serious about partnership schemes and about providing quality teacher education have to commit resources to the scheme. Current arrangements mean that HEIs do transfer funds to schools and so there is 'new' money, in the school's terms, for this work. However, HEIs institutions are clearly losing money and this has long-term implications for the basis of teacher education. In the short term HEIs are just about coping with the new arrangements.

Overall, then, most mentors should be able to undertake the role with some careful preparation, with adequate school and HE support and within a culture of school-based teacher education that recognizes that partnerships require consistent efforts on both sides to create and maintain a quality course for student teachers. Some preparation can be done in-house. For example, mentors can certainly prepare for the role by undertaking the observation of their immediate colleagues and, also, by being observed by them. Such activities are valuable in themselves for everyone involved but they also help the mentor to appreciate the whole experience of observation. Some preparation is best done through in-service provision or courses organized by HEIs. It is worth repeating here that mentors can become involved in interviewing student teachers, hosting pre-course visits, contributing to HEI sessions, writing and reviewing course documentation and running sessions for other mentors as part of HEI meetings. Any decent course will have a number of committees and groups advising on course management and development (see Chapter 1), and these do provide opportunities for personal and professional development.

The simple point is that becoming a good mentor is not easy, and that it is not a position to undertake lightly. There is no reason why a good teacher should become a good mentor: mentoring, like teaching, takes a lot of work and a great deal of thought. It also requires the support of colleagues and of the partnership structure. Many good teachers would be right to turn down the request to take on mentoring: a poor model devalues teaching and devalues the role of the mentor. Even the most thoughtful and experienced mentor, working in a well planned and reasonably resourced partnership scheme, is going to find aspects of mentorship extremely taxing and draining. The next chapter examines the interpersonal side of the mentor–student teacher relationship and is intended to help readers to face the difficulties as well as to enjoy the personal satisfactions of becoming a skilled mentor.

4 Being the mentor: looking after the learning of student teachers of English

Should mentors be student-centred?

There is still little agreement about whether teaching itself should be fundamentally student-centred or knowledge-centred, and both sides of the argument have their advocates. I suspect that most teachers are of the unremarkable
opinion that 'a bit of both' is what is required. I certainly tend towards the
student end of the spectrum, on the basis of the principle that respect for the
individual leads to respect by individuals for other individuals, that principle
ultimately is the basis for democracy. Schools, of course, are not democracies,
but they are highly organized places and so, in my opinion, are good democracies. Freedom takes a good deal of organizing and should never be confused
with either anarchy or 'anything goes'. A democracy wishes to establish the
right level of order to preserve and protect individual freedom. However, a
sense of good order is not the same as giving orders. Teaching is one of those
paradoxical roles in which the best teachers seek constantly to maintain and
promote good order so that children can be free to do well and also free from
the interference and disruptiveness of others. This personally philosophical
aside tells you much about my views of the purpose and value of education
and, not surprisingly, relates to my views about mentoring.

I think that mentoring definitely needs to be located towards the student
end of the spectrum, and I think there is a great deal of evidence to show that
really successful mentoring can only be found in that place. Student teachers
should be respected as individuals. So, in this chapter, I am going to argue the
case for this kind of approach and provide some examples of how it can work
to everyone's advantage. I do think it important to stress, however, that being
very professional and being student-centred are not in conflict. Towards the
end of Chapter 3 I discussed how a mentor will need to make impartial,

professional judgements. I am not implying that professionalism is cold and mechanical; on the contrary, true professionalism is intensely caring and, ironically therefore, being professional is very tough on the individual. Being professional and caring should not be confused with mere liking and disliking. Teachers are comparable in many ways to doctors, nurses and social workers; we all work in caring professions but we certainly do not have to like all the individuals for whom we have some responsibility, or, come to that, all of our colleagues. Being student-centred as a mentor means thinking about how a student teacher is an individual, with individual strengths and weaknesses. All student teachers have chosen, not always wisely, to expose many of these aspects of themselves to a very rigorous challenge. The student-centred mentor respects the student and the challenge.

One final, but very pertinent, point concerns the subject of English. In Chapter 2, I looked briefly at some well known models of the subject, demonstrating that the most popular model operating within English is *personal growth*. This model is, by definition, child-centred, and would appear to offer, for many reasons, a model for mentoring itself. I think it does and it will feature in some of the ideas covered below. As we know, English teachers do define their subject as highly personal, and do have strong views about how working with literature helps the individual, how their attention to language helps to empower pupils and so on. However, our teaching model is by no means the same as our adult interpersonal model. Not only, as we reviewed in Chapter 3, is working with adult learners significantly different to working with children and adolescents, but expert–novice relationships are even more differentiated. In summary, we may operate a very effective personal growth model in the classroom but not be able to bring that, at least initially, to our model of mentorship. We are once more reviewing the demand for self-consciousness in the style of the reflective practitioner. Our subject teaching model may lead us to think that we operate a personal growth approach in all our professional work. This is frequently, and, now that we analyse it, not surprisingly, not always the case. Some student teachers are quite bewildered by observing English teachers whose classroom presence, style and concern for children they can only admire, but whose interaction with adults, and especially student teachers, they find very contrasting.

I am suggesting that the mentoring of all student teachers, regardless of subject, should be properly and professionally student-centred. I am also arguing that English teachers have good reason to suppose that their mentoring approach could be highly effective and that they could draw very valuably on their well established classroom model. This 'advantage' should not, however, be either over-rated or unchallenged: it is just as possible that it may prove a very real disadvantage if not reflected upon with care. This is yet another reason why mentors have a strong case for additional support and for attending courses, because we all need help to reflect. Below I discuss some of the issues connected to being an experienced teacher but, possibly, a novice mentor.

Looked at in this way – that is, as someone starting out on a new role – a good mentor will be the one who recognizes that she is bound to have needs and to benefit from some guidance, even if she is not sure, at this beginning stage, what would help.

Mentoring and skilful caring

I discussed in Chapter 3 the singular problems that spring from the 'teachers are born not made' contingent. I believe that readers of this book are most unlikely to hold such a view, and that they can do a great deal of good by helping to dispel that particular mythology and also by helping student teachers to feel that they really can learn how to be good teachers. I think it more problematic to convince readers about the idea that caring can be 'skilful'. For most people, 'being caring' is not something that receives much conscious attention. By that I do not mean that most people are not caring, I mean that the contexts and situations in which they are most caring are 'natural settings', in the family, the home, with friends, with close colleagues and so on. Readers may say, so far, so obvious.

It is also worth offering another observation here, although I accept that this is a very large generalization. The inhabitants of the United Kingdom are somewhat renowned for their *sang froid*, their coolness and their lack of demonstrativeness. Whether readers accept this point, whether it applies to them personally or not, they may be prepared to accept that British culture is, in some ways, a socially constraining one. This factor is important in mentoring: because student teaching is a highly emotional and frequently stressful business, keeping a 'stiff upper lip' is a particularly difficult and, under certain circumstances, potentially damaging approach. Student teachers are likely to be extremely demonstrative at times and they may well benefit from a calm and reasoned piece of support; just as often they may need a shoulder to cry on, usually metaphorically, but, if my experience is anything to go by, certainly literally at times.

The combination of these two points, one about the ambient culture, the other about our intuitive approach to being caring, means that readers may feel that being asked to 'care professionally' is both artificial and uncomfortable. Teachers frequently comment on how they are expected to be pseudo-parents, pseudo-social workers and the local police, all at the same time. I appreciate that far too much is expected of teachers in a general way, especially given the disrespect shown to the profession by politicians and the media on a daily basis. However, I argue very specifically that caring can be skilful and that it can, to some extent, be learned. To some degree, looking after student teachers is a reasonably obvious extension of the pastoral role accepted by most teachers. However, working with stressed adults, in what is for them a potentially threatening situation, does call on very special skills and attitudes, not just on being a 'naturally' caring person. I also offer this point to those who may feel reluctant to take on the role of mentor because they worry that they may not be supportive enough; part of the point of the rest of the chapter is to review how being supportive can be thoughtful, not just spontaneous.

I shall now to seek to outline how I think any mentor may approach being a skilled carer while happily accepting that this is a part of the role that mentors may feel rather cautious about and may prefer to 'grow into' with experience. To examine this area, I am going to review some influential ideas, mostly from psychology, that fall loosely under the heading of counselling. A final point to make before I begin this process is to reassure the reader that *being a mentor is not the same as being a counsellor* and that I do not pretend for a moment that reading this chapter will provide anything like enough material for someone to become a counsellor. Most modern counselling takes a very non-interventionist approach, (I shall say more below about this), and mentors, for all the numerous points outlined above, are constantly and systematically intervening. Counselling is an aspect of mentoring, and one that I believe we need to consider more fully in school-based teacher education.

Supporting student teachers

Over the past 150 years psychology has provided us with many insights that continue to help us to make sense of human behaviour, but, despite these advances, we have as yet fully to understand ourselves.[1] Psychology is therefore something with a great deal to offer anyone working with people, but without ever making the claim of being an exact science. A mentor can draw on these psychological insights and apply them without having to feel that she is responsible for someone else's personality. The most useful starting point for us comes from what is usually termed humanistic psychology.[2] This approach originates chiefly from the work of American psychologists such as George Kelly, Abraham Maslow and Carl Rogers. They challenged Freud's obsessions, as they saw it, with the negative aspects of human behaviour. In Freudian psychology much human behaviour can seem relentlessly fixed and driven. Until we resolve deep rooted problems we cannot break free to true adulthood and a balanced sense of self. Much of Freud's work remains very important, but perhaps more in the treatment of the abnormal than the ordinary. Some readers may find some of their colleagues, and a few student teachers, somewhat abnormal, but that should be the subject of a different book.

Humanistic psychology is much more useful to us because it operates from the concept that most human behaviour comes from positive impulses and that individuals can take control of their destiny. This concept 'fits' closely with what most people believe about education, and the role of the teacher in particular, which is to help children become positive adults. However, it also posits the idea that reality is something we constantly *construct*. Our understanding of the world really is the world that we inhabit. This idea can easily be over-simplified and parodied ('So you're telling me that the table over there looks different to you from the one I see?'), but when considered at a sophisticated level, this notion of construction really helps us to help ourselves and each other. We are constructing the world because we want to *understand it*, because we have a positive wish to make sense of what we see and what we do; we want our contribution to be *meaningful*.

This basic premise, that we are positively constructing the world, has led many psychologists, theoretical and clinical, to place increasing emphasis on a model of *counselling rather than curing*. I think most readers will already be clear that much of the emphasis of this book is on helping student teachers to learn, not merely telling them what to do. We have already examined how too much telling can reduce the capacity of the individual to undertake thoughtful, independent action. A mentor is not a counsellor but a counselling model offers tremendous help and insight. Carl Rogers in particular (see note 2) developed a *facilitative* model. This starts from the point I outlined above of a basic respect for the individual. The stance to take is that of basic acceptance, of 'unconditional positive regard', providing a warm receptiveness without placing demands and expectations on the individual. Before readers express the impossibility of such saint-like behaviour, let me put this in its full context. In order to 'get to know' someone and to have an understanding of her views and feelings, one needs not just sympathy, but what is termed an 'accurate empathy'. Our language is full of common sayings about this concept; perhaps 'stepping into someone's shoes', is a helpful example, as it implies not just seeing the world from her point of view but also feeling it, experiencing how it feels to her. This is a perfectly ordinary human action, seeing someone else's point of view. Readers are fully aware that this is not actually easy and that some humans seem to find it impossible. However, that we all make this attempt, at least some of the time, and that it is an action comprehensible to reasonable adults, is important in stressing that it is well within the remit of any reasonable adult, not just saint-like figures.

A mentor is seeking to bring the best out of an individual student and to help her make the right kind of impact in the classroom. As student teachers bring many assumptions, expectations and attitudes to school experience, so we need to know what these are, to identify which ones may help and which ones may hinder the students' success with children's learning and, very importantly, in establishing relationships with professional colleagues. A student teacher may need considerable help to bring these factors to a conscious level and to articulate them in such a way as to begin to understand their force. So through initially offering an accepting stance, a mentor can provide a helpful and friendly space for the student to articulate and then examine her ideas. I have discussed at great length already how essential it is for student teachers to articulate their beliefs about the subject of English (and other things) and to engage in thoughtful, open discussion about them. I have tried to show that this is an eminently *practical* idea; it helps the student and it helps the mentor to help the student.

However, some readers may still be feeling frustrated at the prospect of sitting back and smiling while students offer one 'daft' idea after another. This picture would once more be of saints and not reasonable adults. The first point is that, although a mentor may have huge amounts to offer a student and could 'soon put her right', most of this knowledge would simply be overwhelming, especially when the student lacks the experiential framework to understand it. By an experiential framework, I mean that the more successful experiences she has had, the more she will be susceptible and open to sophisticated advice. So careful listening by the mentor helps tremendously because it allows for the selection of what will be helpful to the learner, *now and in the future*.

Equally, if we are hearing a 'daft' idea, and we all have, it does not mean that we simply smile and go along with it. Using a counselling approach means that first we do not say, dismissively, 'That is a daft idea and will lead to a disastrous lesson! How can you be so stupid?' It does mean, however, that we want to show the student teacher that we do not agree with what she is planning to do and that it is the *plans* that we are unhappy with, not the person. This approach helps us to retain our sense of self, our genuine views; we are not compromising our principles. We do not pretend to agree with a student teacher to make her feel good, least of all when she is setting up trouble for herself. To sum up, we start by accepting what she offers as a genuine attempt to do well and then we try to get at what she is trying to do and why she thinks it will succeed. Having established this positive basis, we can then *examine the plan critically*, keeping the focus on the plan and its likely effects. The student teacher can then be critical of the plan in collaboration with the mentor, seeking to review and revise it but still to have *responsibility* for it. We will need to return to this basic idea and explore it more fully, especially as, I believe, it helps to explain why case study approaches are so valuable in learning how to teach. Some readers may still feel that this is far too 'softly, softly' an approach, and I hope to show how a mentor's individual judgement will necessarily refine and temper the approach. Before moving on, I should like to stress once more that 'accurate empathy', means *being accurate and judging acutely*; it has nothing to do with giving students a false image of themselves or their progress. Getting the balance right between encouragement and negative criticism is, of course, extremely difficult for all of us; hence the need for devoting a considerable proportion of this chapter to exploring those difficulties and to offering some ways of dealing with the issue.

I think it crucial here to acknowledge that an implicit element in this approach can be summed up in very everyday terms as 'patience'. What goes with patience is time. Schools and teachers are notoriously short of time and always have been. The arrival of the National Curriculum, whatever its other positive advantages, has exacerbated this problem enormously. Contrary to certain views, HEI tutors are short of time too; I offer this point not to attract sympathy, but simply to point up how we – that is, everyone collaborating now in teacher education – are very much in the same hectic boat. The chief point is that, as with all other aspects of learning, there must be an allocation of time for that learning, and that it will never really be enough, but that we do get remarkably skilful at making the most of limited time. A mentor who invests time in listening, especially early on in the student's time in school, is likely, I would argue, to save potentially vast amounts of time later on. The temptation for all of us, we experts in charge of novices, is to talk to them, to tell them what it is all about. Common sense seems to demand that we fill up their empty heads with readily available wisdom, and *the students want this too*. They are desperate to have the certainties that they think we have.

However, uncommon sense helps us to see that some patient listening will establish a level of personal, professional partnership that is the basis for long-term development. Finally, patient listening confers respect and value on the speaker and gives her some status, even when she generally feels without it, and this leads us on to a vital element in student teachers' development, their whole concept of status.

Student teachers and status

In this chapter we have been examining ideas about looking after student teachers from a more pastoral perspective, but always with the appropriate focus on helping them to become good teachers. I feel that this concept needs a good deal more elaboration and support, and want to look now at an issue that helps us to begin that elaboration.

Abraham Maslow (see note 2) developed a theory of needs that has been highly influential and gives us a useful insight into the particular nature of the student teacher's experience. Maslow's concept is that, although we have a range of needs that we experience at all times, some are more basic and fundamental than others. In terms of level, it will not surprise readers to know that our physical needs and our sense of safety come first; unless we have these, we may not be able to concentrate on other levels or be much concerned about higher order needs. If we have our basic needs met then we go on to higher orders, such as needing acceptance by others and belonging to a group. Once we begin to belong, we move higher, needing to be valued so that we are prepared to contribute and from this position to strive for esteem and respect. Eventually, if we are really secure and confident then we are prepared to be different, to take risks and to be original. Of course, such a broad concept cannot match all human beings or behaviours; nor does Maslow suggest that it does. First, it is useful as a rule of thumb approach to almost any learning situation, and student teachers on most HE courses are encouraged to think about its implications for their classrooms. Second, the fact that we can all think of many exceptional individuals who seem able to surmount this hierarchy of needs and overcome it helps to show how our ordinary humanity is something that we usefully have in common. We all share these needs. Knowing where to find the toilets is a strong desire that new pupils, new members of staff, new student teachers and visiting HE tutors all have in common; exceptional individuals with superhuman bladders are much to be admired but are rare.

The third point is that Maslow's hierarchy is extremely helpful when we are thinking about supporting adults in stressful situations. Beginning teaching is usually extremely stressful. Some of this stress is necessary and even of use, but if student teachers never escape from a constant sense of insecurity they are unlikely to move up that ladder of needs to a point where they can contribute much of value.

Let me illustrate with the issue of status and begin with something so simple that it is not always addressed: the naming of parts. Most partnership handbooks are full of carefully defined terminology to describe the people fulfilling key roles. For example, subject mentors can also be 'supervising teachers' or 'cooperating teachers'; student teachers can also be 'interns'. However, what is a student teacher actually to be called in the classroom? It may be difficult to convince readers of the vehemence with which student teachers, especially early in the course, denounce some teachers for their 'appalling' behaviour. Some quotations may help:

> I was incensed. She said to the class, 'Here are a couple of students from the university, just ignore them.'

> Not once in the whole day did anyone introduce me to any class, I sat there like an idiot.

> And then he said 'Ask *the girls* to help you as well.' and he meant us. I haven't been called a girl for ten years!

> One of them said to the class, 'They aren't inspectors or anything, just a couple of students from somewhere or other.'

> I spent the whole morning in the staffroom and not one person spoke to me.

> He introduced us as 'A couple of students who may be unlucky enough to have to try and teach you.' How are we supposed to have any status now?

> One man, who had never seen me before in his life, actually started to tell me off in the corridor for not being in the sixth form study area.

Readers will recognize in these quotations the mismatch between the teachers' off-hand, usually well intentioned remarks and actions, and the student teachers' hypersensitivities.

Students do, of course, recover from all this angst, but it is genuine enough. One of the very great advantages of school-based teacher education is that students become 'like regular teachers'. From their point of view, becoming as familiar as the wallpaper is a great advantage. However, the point about names, and therefore status, is an important one for a mentor, who needs to make student teachers feel secure so that they will want to belong to the department and to the school. It really does help enormously if student teachers are introduced formally, *as teachers*, and if this approach is adopted consistently across the school. Because of their insecurities, student teachers are quite likely to over-react, especially to anything that appears to threaten their very fragile status. Most teachers have forgotten how long it takes to acquire status in the school and in the classroom, and how precious it is. Experienced teachers are habituated to it and, with many other things, lose sight of it. I really do not think that being upset about one's name or one's status is of any use to anyone; one learns nothing from it. Learning to teach brings many humiliations without someone adding to them in order to make sure that student teachers feel at the bottom of the heap; they feel that already. Every pupil in the school appears to know more about what matters than a student teacher. It seems to me, then, that a mentor can do a great deal with *relatively little effort* to initiate a student teacher in such a way as to begin a positive process of status building and security. In case any reader feels that this author protests too much, out of a sense of self-importance, about this issue of status, let me reassure you that HEI tutors when visiting schools are accorded very little. As for names, some student teachers are soon as guilty as the rest. I have sat in many a classroom without a reference to my existence by anyone except the occasional child's enquiry, not usually after my well-being either. A few children have been grateful for my reasonable ability at spelling and have been impressed enough to ask my name. Overall, most student teachers do introduce me and we discuss before the lesson what they will call me and where I will sit. I have my own needs too and it certainly helps my security to know how to behave appropriately in someone else's classroom.

Throughout the book we have been examining general approaches that always need contextualization and active differentiation by mentors to match them to a student teacher's development. On this issue of status and security it is worth looking at this generally in relation to one statistically significant group of students. A considerable proportion of student teachers of all subjects, but especially of English, are 'mature'. For a university any student over 26 is mature, but I am focusing much more specifically on students over 30. The great majority of this group, as is true of English teachers nationally, are female. I think it worth emphasizing, in a broad way, some characteristics of this group, as a group. Ultimately, the principle of their individuality is not compromised by suggesting that they may have generalizable needs to some extent.

Maturity and experience are a double-edged sword. They provide many positive aspects, often including parenthood, which are generally seen by most teachers, and usually the student teachers themselves, as helpful. Often their experience includes considerable work experience of other contexts and of responsibilities that provide a very useful platform for starting to teach. Some mature students have selected teaching despite highly successful careers elsewhere, sometimes where high salaries, company cars and extensive benefits were the norm. Others may have taken a late degree, particularly when children are becoming more independent, and have chosen English teaching for a whole range of reasons, convenience sometimes being one.

All these students can be described as 'mature'. Some have had very high status, others, in their own terms at least, relatively low status. For all of them, even those who are choosing teaching despite other successes, starting teaching is at least as stressful as for 'young' students. For many it is actually *far more* stressful. First, all student teachers, as discussed above, feel that they have very low status. Second, we must accept that many staff quite definitely reinforce this idea, and should they meet a student teacher who is confident, articulate and intelligently critical they may not adopt the best reflective practitioner approach; on the contrary, they may simply use their own status to overwhelm the student. Without becoming at all stereotypical, I would have to say that, in my experience, mature women students are much more likely to receive this treatment than any other student teacher, and they are just as likely to receive it from female as male staff. I include in my definition of 'staff' all of us working in partnership schemes, not just colleagues in school. Third, such students frequently have extensive responsibilities, usually in the home, already, and often experience quite intense pressures and feelings of guilt about neglecting these responsibilities. Fourth, if you are mature, experienced and well prepared, you ought to do well in teaching, but if you are not doing well the cost of failure is very high indeed. Failing, or even just struggling, as a teacher is usually a very public and therefore extremely humiliating experience. Sometimes this struggle may be worsened by pressures from home, where there is little understanding and much criticism. I am painting a bleak scenario indeed, but one based on many genuine examples. To sum up, a mentor may find that a mature student imports a tremendous amount into starting teaching but this is no guarantee of her eventual success. In general terms, some of the very best student teachers that I have worked with in English, and many other subjects, have been mature, but rather more have had a difficult time; many of the students who have had most trouble with learning to teach have been mature. Mature students may, for all these reasons, need particularly sensitive handling and I hope that this section has reinforced the point about how using counselling models can be a highly effective part of mentoring.

Can there be a challenge without stress?

A mentor has to work with various levels of stress. Teaching is a demanding and stressful activity and so, at times is mentoring, but much of the time both activities become consistently successful and enjoyable. For student teachers almost everything they face is a challenge. A challenge is, essentially, a good thing, because we can accept it as such; for student teachers, the temptation is to accept *every* challenge in order to show willing and to prove themselves. Such an approach is worthy but, ultimately, mistaken. One of the benefits of experience is a modicum of wisdom, allowing the individual to make judgements about the likelihood of success. A mentor is also a mediator, coming between the student and her aspirations, to temper those aspirations, so that they can be engaged in successful outcomes. As we were considering above, the students' motives are basically sound and good: to get involved, to prove themselves in the classroom, to help children learn and so on. The problem lies in their perception of what is achievable. Here is a classic case where a mentor can acknowledge, celebrate and praise students' motivation but make it clear that, offering advice as an experienced teacher, there are better ways of achieving the desired goal.

Student teachers have no shortage of stress, and most mentors need to reduce it when they can. The right degree of stress is valuable, as it energizes and stimulates us. We tend to experience stress when facing the new and unfamiliar. Novelty is generally exciting and stimulating and, being new, there is a degree of uncertainty attached to it. There is plenty of evidence to show that we all need regular stimulation and that a degree of novelty is important for our sense of well-being; the opposite, when things become merely routine and boring, leads to all kinds of problems. Teaching, as readers will be aware, is no exception. An important aside here is that the role of mentoring may be initially attractive because of its challenge and novelty. However, becoming a successful mentor will involve balancing this challenge element with a growing sense of certainty and secure professional knowledge. If our school-based partnership model settles into being the norm, we shall need to review what our challenges should be. I deal with some ideas related to this point in the next two chapters.

The basic point for a mentor to consider is not, usually, whether these student teachers are being challenged, but whether they are being over-stretched and, possibly, damaged by their current difficulties. There is the issue of challenge when a student teacher is becoming consciously competent, and I shall return to this idea later in the chapter.

The mentor as protector

We examined in Chapter 3 how students tend to go through certain phases in learning to teach and how the mentor can skilfully manage this process of development, helping the student to move from progressively collaborative teaching to increasingly independent teaching. We concentrated in one section on students' very proper desire to get stuck in, to get into the action.

All students have difficulties, especially with being in the action. Even the few remarkably effective student teachers that I have worked with have faced some challenges that threatened to overwhelm them. In my own case, I remember well that my teaching practice was very demanding and wore me out, although it bore little comparison to the first two years that I taught in what used to be called a social priority school. I was constantly overwhelmed there and frequently at a loss as to how manage certain pupils and certain aspects of pupils' learning. I had many supportive colleagues around me and, however daunting it was at times, I loved the job. There was not much formal support, however, and my colleagues had many pressures to deal with. I certainly felt unsure of how to make the most of what support and advice was available. Moreover, like many other 'qualified' teachers, I had a certificate proclaiming that I could 'do the job'. I was undertaking a probationary year but this was really, as I remember it, a formality. I felt some constraint then in admitting, at times, that I was struggling desperately with some children. Having the courage to face up to what looks, and feels, like failure is very difficult and I remember my own context vividly. If I had asked for more help I would have put myself through less distress and learnt to be a reasonable teacher a good deal more quickly.

This illustration from my own teaching career is intended to highlight one of the very considerable advantages of school-based teacher education, but one that relies, very heavily, on a mentor's dedication to that role. As I have emphasized several times, I believe that well managed partnership schemes can prepare student teachers very effectively for a career in teaching. One element to focus on now is how mentors can intervene in the struggle that all student teachers face in learning to teach. Some students, as readers will know well, struggle throughout the course, and, almost inevitably, are those that are hardest to help, sometimes being apparently immune to advice. In this section we need to look at the signs of distress and what we can do, within the limits of our resources and our responsibility. Contrary to popular opinion, a considerable number of students drop out of courses, or are failed. This is an unhappy situation, but it is, without question, the best outcome for the individuals concerned and for the profession. Such students often, unwittingly, cause the maximum stress in others, as well as themselves, and may absorb huge amounts of support and professional time. It seems to me, under current selection procedures, and probably under any, that there will always be a small percentage of student teachers who become increasingly problematic in school, and that we have a collaborative job to do in recognizing that no system involving human beings can be perfect.

For the great majority of students, the challenges and difficulties they face are highly productive for learning; they are so highly motivated that they cope with all kinds of strain and stress and still, as the folk wisdom puts it, 'keep smiling'. However, there is a danger even in coping strategies that a mentor needs to watch.

The initial consideration is simply that some degree of distress or negative feelings is typical, and, to a large extent, inevitable. I would be alarmed by a student who constantly said 'There are no problems,' and will discuss that kind of defensiveness below, but most students do not want to admit *the extent* of their negative feelings. One great advantage of adopting the positive stance of the counselling model is that it genuinely encourages a student teacher to be honest and to confront her own distress. A mentor needs to make the student recognize that it is good (and normal) to feel bad. It is not an admission of failure; on the contrary, it is a sign of growth and often a necessary part of the learning process. Let us look at what tends to happen if a student teacher refuses to acknowledge her 'bad feelings'.

One may be stimulated by a reasonable amount of challenge but when one is overwhelmed one simply feels confusion and danger, the equivalent to panic. During a feeling of panic, one is unable to do anything reflective. One simply reacts, instinctively, to what the situation seems to demand. Later it may be very hard to admit to such 'foolishness', let alone to learn anything from what happened. What has happened is that we have lost some capacity to learn from the situation and will need a great deal of help to revisit that highly stressful time and to analyse it. It is not just that panic and anxiety make us unreceptive to learning; they may actually knock us back so that we lose some of the valuable recent learning we have acquired. This point is yet one more piece of evidence against the sink or swim school of 'thought'.

In the classroom this sense of panic leads to 'instinctive' but really regressive behaviours. Without a moment's thought a student may suddenly start shouting at a pupil or a whole class, having stated categorically that she will never 'shout at children'. She may threaten children with all kinds of punishments and sanctions that bear little relation to the discipline sanctions of the school. I accept, very readily, that this is a very typical occurrence, but so are car accidents, and we do not set those up or keep repeating them because, eventually, we learn to avoid them. In a sense what happens *later* is the key element.

For many people, defensiveness is an initial reaction whenever a threat is perceived. If a student feels that she is about to be 'attacked' for what she has done, perhaps even feels that she *deserves* to be attacked, then an automatic, and usually therefore unconscious, response is to be defensive. Verbally this tends to take the form either of aggressiveness or of apportioning blame to everyone but the self. The mentor is therefore already in a tricky position. This defensive stance is not triggered by the mentor or even by some neutral question like 'How did it go?' It is, instead, an *automatic, unreflective reaction*. A mentor may be able to recognize this reaction for what it is and so try to move the student teacher out of this defensive position to a more objective one, where it would be possible to construct a strategy. However, it is important to recognize that some people are extremely practised and tenacious in their defensive stance; perhaps in the past it has been a successful way of avoiding confronting difficult aspects of their lives, whether working or personal. If a student teacher begins to adopt such a stance consistently then there is no question that there are going to be real problems. A mentor is no longer dealing solely with learning about teaching, but with a much more confused situation.

Defensiveness can take a number of forms, and some of them look less like defensiveness than others. In every case, though, they offer a mentor some warning signs. It is perhaps worth remembering that for some students this may only be a phase, frequently induced by them taking on more than they are ready for. By reading these signs a mentor might review the current load on a student and, by relatively minor adjustments, help her to move forward again.

One aspect of defensiveness, as with the shouting at the class mentioned above, is impulsive reaction. Perhaps a student might say, 'Oh well if you are going to drag up that problem again there is no point in going on,' even followed by some withdrawing action like resolutely looking away or walking off. The reaction may simply be anger and distress. A more subtle, and harder to interpret, reaction is to seem too busy to be concerned, perhaps pouring masses of energy into producing materials without actually thinking about what difference this use of time may make. Then, when all the work is laboriously finished, and the mentor expresses concern that the class in question may not 'appreciate' all this work, the student can throw up her hands and say 'What can I do then?', but without wanting to hear the advice. Many readers may recognize this syndrome from friends and family or from themselves. When upset we often busy ourselves with something straightforward and routine to displace the anxiety we feel; in certain circumstances this may be helpful, in the short term, but a student teacher almost always has to face the cause of stress again very soon, and the busyness, in this context, is actually a waste of time.

A much more obvious element of defensiveness is a form of refusal to see what is happening. After a difficult experience a student may apparently have selected the difficult part out, or may try to deflect attention: 'Yes, but they really liked the video at the end, didn't they?' Once more a mentor, using the counselling model, can begin by accepting such points, but eventually it may become clear that the student is actually *refusing to accept* what she is consciously aware was happening. Further tactics may be used: wandering off the point; trying to switch back to something else from the past or from the present, where the mentor will have to agree that things are, or were, all right. Sometimes it is as simple as avoidance, or basic procrastination: 'I will get round to that tomorrow.'

One of the most uncomfortable defensive modes is blaming everyone and everything else, a kind of *reattribution* which can often involve very elaborate interpretations of what went on to make this convincing. This style of defensiveness tends to have particular aspects not always operating at the same time, sometimes used to switch to when one approach is not convincing the listener. A student may construct a very rational sounding reason for what happened, but the mentor will see immediately that, however *plausible*, this is not the actual reason for the problem. Equally, a student may simply emphasize that the other elements, not the student, somehow failed; for example, 'I did everything just as you said I should, but they were simply not interested and that story that the head of department recommended was really difficult, they hated it.' And so it goes on. The mentor faces a confused situation where the student keeps shifting ground, so that any useful analysis is hard to attempt.

One of the very worst situations involves the student who simply cannot see any problems. According to these student teachers, they have absorbed all the advice given to them, applied it in their work and seen it producing results. For example, such a student might say, 'I had them working in pairs, then they moved into groups and finally they did some individual work, just as you are always saying it should happen.' In fact, the children may have been sitting in pairs attempting a poorly thought through task, then have been moved into groups with no real purpose, and, as yet, with nothing to say about the so-called task, and then been separated just as they were sorting out something useful by pooling their ideas. The student then attributes all the blame for a poor lesson to a classroom approach she actually does not believe in and has clearly never tried out properly. Even so, she sees no problem with this lesson: 'Didn't I do what was expected of me?' Mentors and HEI tutors find these student teachers extremely difficult to help. Some of these students are from that small percentage who eventually are deemed not competent. A few, through the patience and support of their host department and their HEI tutor, may eventually respond to advice; sometimes they only become more receptive when the likelihood of failure is spelt out. This does not contradict the earlier points about mentors listening and using 'accurate empathy'. These students are the ones who are least self aware and who only recognize their limitations after constant, and often very direct, comments about those limitations. As I have stressed, they have first to accept responsibility for what is happening in the classroom and with their colleagues.

As I have tried to emphasize throughout, these generalizations are useful in helping us to deal with individuals, all of whom have differences and distinctions. Equally, the intense nature of learning to teach does mean that students can move quite rapidly through phases and so can 'come through' a difficult patch and emerge far more settled and receptive to advice and support.

I should like to conclude this section with a related but rather different kind of challenge, the unusually successful student. It is one major premise of this book that learning to teach is extremely difficult and that helping to learn requires a great deal of careful thought and considerable resources. I also made the point above that even the most immediately 'successful' student teachers go through considerable difficulties. However, the very best student teachers tend to be thoughtful and reflective, critical in the open-minded sense, reasonably confident but also strongly self-critical, quick to blame themselves, and not others, for problems and extremely receptive to advice and constructive criticism. In a good partnership scheme, such students flourish. An important aside here is that for mentors who are looking after a pair of students, the 'other' student may, of course, feel very unsuccessful in comparison; this only becomes a real problem, however, if comparisons are made.

With an exceptional student the mentor faces a different challenge from the norm. Perhaps after only a few weeks of such a student teacher's main practice, she is already clearly competent and beginning to make a very considerable contribution to the department; perhaps even trying out successfully some things that more experienced staff have yet to do, such as using IT. One, understandable, reaction might be 'Congratulations, you have made it,' followed, metaphorically, by the mentor walking away; after all, there is no shortage of things to get on with in a busy English department. However, no good teacher would do this with her class, i.e. simply ignore them because they are doing well. There is some evidence, however, that teachers in general find it more difficult to know what to do to support and extend the most able. Some research with English teachers themselves, and their pupils, has shown this to be a significant concern within English itself (Goodwyn, 1995).

I hope that these initial points are helpful to mentors in once more showing that there is nothing 'automatic' in the situation. Knowing how to challenge the best student teachers is not a 'natural' part of the mentor's role and nor does it involve just doing 'more of the same'. It requires thoughtful and planned intervention even more consciously than with a more 'typical' student. This is especially true because such a student may arrive at a plateau, relatively early on. It may be a high plateau, but it is not in her interest, or the children's, for her to spend too long there.

In my own experience, the combined expertise of the HEI tutor and the mentor can be focused on such a student's particular needs and a properly differentiated programme can easily be negotiated. I am not suggesting that a mentor cannot independently negotiate such a programme with her student, I am simply describing what we all felt was a valuable collaboration and a very positive aspect of partnership. I do not think as yet that we have paid enough attention to these kinds of students, partly, of course, because they are relatively rare and they also tend to be so independent. It is an exciting prospect to think that we might be able to learn together, in partnership, about challenging these exceptional students.

Mentors and self-esteem

I drew the distinction earlier between skilful caring and personal liking, and I also commented on the idea that demands on mentors may sometimes feel so great that a halo would be the only appropriate reward. However, we all have to work with student teachers (and colleagues) whom we find difficult. The mentor–mentee relationship could become, in this respect, one of the most problematic of professional relationships.

Many years ago, when taking my own PGCE course, I read for the first time James Britton's great work *Language and Learning* (Britton, 1970). I learned many things from this seminal text, although it took me many more years to put some of its ideas, all too inadequately, into practice. I was very impressed on my first reading with some points he made about professional relationships. His emphasis was principally on the teacher–pupil relationship, but I feel that the point made is extremely helpful in offering a model for the mentor–mentee relationship. He draws initially on the work of Clare Winnicott, whose focus is the social worker. He quotes this section:

> Our professional relationships are more balanced and more reliable than our personal ones, and it is important that they should be. We look to our *personal* relationships for the satisfaction of our personal *need* for relationships – for in-stinct satisfaction. (By instinct satisfaction I mean the need to love and be loved in a personal intimate way.) Personal relationships are, therefore, less reliable because they are subject to our needs and demands, to our moods and our jealousies and rivalries.
>
> (Winnicott, 1964: 12)

He goes on to elaborate this point and explains that such an approach allows 'clients' themselves (in social work terms) to be personal within the profes-sional relationship because they are investing themselves into it. The profes-sional is trying to create 'a limited and reliable environment' (Britton, 1970: 183) so that the 'clients' can grow and develop. This, I would suggest, is very much what a mentor is trying to establish for a student teacher. The benefit to the mentor is in the way this professional relationship provides value and self-esteem. Britton quotes from Winnicott again:

> we get a fundamental reassurance about our value and our goodness – because people can take and use what we give. We get the chance to contribute to the world through our professional function and thereby relate ourselves to society and feel more secure in it . . . this is a very great deal, and fundamental to our well-being and our ability to do our work.
>
> (Winnicott, 1964: 12)

I am still not suggesting that teachers in general are the same as social workers or that, in becoming a mentor, one automatically becomes one. How-ever, there is a clear similarity in the nature of the reward that Winnicott and Britton are suggesting comes from being truly professional. I feel that it is crucial for a mentor to recognize that the true reward in mentoring is chiefly altruistic. When one carries out an altruistic function the principal reward is in enhanced self-esteem and in feeling the value of making a special and distinct contribution. Inevitably, then, I am stressing that mentoring demands certain professional responsibilities and attitudes that require of us a great deal of consistency and patience that we might well not be capable of, as Winnicott helps us to accept, with our family and friends.

It is important to consider this definition of the professional relationship here because many of the issues that we have covered in this chapter, about the challenge to student teachers caused by novelty, uncertainty, stress and panic, certainly might apply to a mentor. Even if someone who is both a highly experienced English teacher and familiar with student teachers volunteers for mentoring, the new, considerably extended role arising from school-based teacher education may come as a very real shock. Indeed, as I have argued in relation to mature student teachers, the combination of teaching experience and familiarity may make it particularly hard to deal with areas where the individual's expertise, so very evident in every other aspect of work, feels weak or non-existent.

In this section I am stressing first that mentors are taking on a role that is very demanding personally; that is, that it will draw extensively on our inner resources as people, while simultaneously requiring of us a kind of professionalism that keeps our personal needs in the background. Of, course, much teaching is exactly like this, but looking after a student teacher more or less all day, every working day, for many months is significantly different to normal teaching. Second, although a mentor may have all the right experience and very positive motives for taking on the role, she may still be a novice in the field; exactly like a student teacher. It is possible, looking at a worst case scenario, for two novices (one the student, but the other the mentor) to be put together who have little in common personally, with differing views about what the relationship entails and a resulting sense of mutual failure. For the mentor this sense of failure may be heavily reinforced by the feeling that she, as the senior partner with overall responsibility, has been unable to put to good use all that teaching experience, subject knowledge and general school know-how. It is certainly worth reviewing here how mentors can help themselves to be wise before and during the event, rather than after it is too late.

The first consideration may well be identifying to what extent the mentoring role is at the right level of challenge. I think a mentor, even an experienced one, will tend to face the prospect of one, or more, demanding student teachers with some proper apprehension. Both the mentoring task and the prospect of new students carry a stimulating element of novelty and uncertainty. This is also a very valuable professional stimulus. Most partnership courses have developed procedures, properly agreed by the HEI and all the schools involved, whereby student teachers are expected to be intelligently critical, and, as well as asking how to do something, they will also be asking why things are carried out in a particular way. This should be a professional stimulus because it does challenge current practice, and many departments that I have worked with say that, despite all the demands that school-based teacher education makes on them, this single factor is the most valuable (see Chapter 1).

However, student teachers are not often skilled at challenging current practice, and what they say, and the way they say it, may simply sound like 'challenge'. For example, suppose that a student says, 'Why do you never ask the girls any questions?' A mentor may, perhaps unconsciously, adopt a defensive stance when handling an especially clumsy question like that, and respond, quite understandably: 'When you have seen a few more of my lessons you will see that I am extremely careful to be fair.' The student has certainly been clumsy and made a rather crude assumption, but the mentor can respond quite differently and more purposefully. First, adopting the positive, but relatively neutral, stance she might respond: 'That is an interesting and challenging point. Tell me more about what you observed.' I feel that this response might lead into a much more productive dialogue, especially if, as might be the case, it is worth following up. As one mentor put it,

> Both the students asked me at different times about the amount of time I was devoting to a few boys – now I felt a bit taken aback by this but then I already knew really that this was a bit of a problem but, once they had pointed it out and we had talked about it, I felt it was time to do something. Over several weeks I worked on this and then I asked them to come in and monitor a couple of lessons. Not only did they say things were more even but they said they had learned some useful strategies for being fairer themselves – but the real gain was for me.

A mentor will have to model open-mindedness and the ability to make use of criticism, especially when, as in this case, the student's basic motivation is perfectly sound.

A connected, and equally valid, point can be illustrated with another representative student remark. Let us suppose the student begins with, 'You know the way you always put your head on one side and look really serious when you answer questions? Well, why do you do that?' It is very possible that no one has ever remarked on this 'habit' before and that it is, to the mentor, an entirely unconscious piece of body language that, for several successful years, has been conveying to pupils that a genuine question is serious and highly valued. As a direct question about one's personal habits, it may be rather shocking and uncomfortable and, initially, unanswerable. However, it is actually an astute piece of observation and worth discussing. The mentor may not be sure how to discuss it, however. We examined at length in Chapter 3 how expertise leads to much of our daily activity becoming habitual and, increasingly, unconscious. This habituation makes it very difficult to articulate what is going on; it requires a great effort of self-consciousness and self-awareness that is not 'normal' human behaviour. Many teachers are highly skilled at teaching and talking to pupils, but relatively unskilled, as we have considered already, at talking about teaching, especially to novices. The mentor, in the case of the body language question, may genuinely need help to be able to stand back from her successful routines and consciously understand them. This, like the initial and rather innocent question, may cause some embarrassment. Most people, in very ordinary situations, feel threatened if they are 'watched'. 'Don't watch me do X or I won't be able to do it,' is probably something we have all said or heard.

My main point is that a mentor is, and should be, exposing herself to intense and minute observation of a genuinely critical kind. Initially, especially from a relative stranger, this is difficult. The mentor may only gradually be able to become skilfully articulate about teaching, and her own teaching in particular. Equally, she may find interpreting a student's well intentioned, but rather threatening questions, very uncomfortable at first. In both ways the professional needs to create that 'limited but reliable environment' in which the student's 'challenge' can be properly sustained and accepted. Part of this limiting, which the mentor properly provides, is to *explain simply*, rather like you might to beginners in other situations. The particular skill of the mentor can be to offer this simplicity in a positive and not a patronizing manner; for example, by beginning 'I find it hard to explain some aspects of teaching, so let me start with what I know and you help me with questions when you want more detail . . .'

We return here to the mentor's patient and positive approach, outlined in some detail above. Student teachers, in my experience, fairly regularly irritate, annoy and even upset highly experienced teachers who are trying their hardest to help the students in question. I think it unlikely, as I am sure readers do too, that this aspect of human behaviour can be entirely eradicated. Most students have no intention of threatening the esteem or value of their mentors; on the contrary they are usually desperate to please and impress them. If the occasional student is trying to challenge that esteem, then I see no reason why the mentor should not be properly angry. I know of one 'mature' student teacher who in her first encounter with her experienced, but actually younger, mentor, when asked if she wanted to discuss classroom management, took a hefty tome out of her bag and said conclusively, 'I did my MA dissertation on that.' Fortunately, the mentor in question was not only a good one but one with a resilient sense of humour.

I can certainly think of a few other student teachers who have been negatively challenging, some quite unconsciously, but others quite deliberately. Such behaviour is simply bad and extremely unprofessional. Sometimes the intervention of a third party, the school's professional tutor perhaps or a relevant HEI tutor, can be a useful and productive strategy. I have, on a single (long) day, met the student, then the mentor, then the student again, then the mentor again, before we all, finally, sat down together.

These difficulties fall within the usual parameters of the situation, but they are still quite exceptional. Mentors are, generally, highly esteemed, properly respected and valued by a range of colleagues and by student teachers. Here are a few comments from students:

She is faultless, wonderful, an absolute professional, I was so lucky to have her support.

He was brilliant, always organized but so flexible, never dogmatic but always ready to offer on the spot advice. He was always planning ahead, never missed a weekly meeting and he made it clear that this was protected time. He was genuinely interested in my views and so I had a real sense of responsibility, what I said and did really mattered to him – if he disagreed he would say so but only so as to make me think more about things.

I was really privileged. The whole department was thoughtful and helpful, it was a real model as a learning environment. All important decisions were negotiated and this made such a difference to both of us [a pair of students]. We could not have had a better mentor.

She was always pushing and nudging me forward but never so that I felt pushed, just what I needed, and if I had been the sort to hold back she would have done that equally carefully.

My mentor, however busy, always made me feel that our time was valuable and so I had to come prepared and I learned so much from that relationship and from having a chance to get into some depth.

I could provide many more examples of the true appreciation that the majority of student teachers have for their mentors. Readers will be pleased to know that the mentors who are most praised are the most experienced *as mentors*. However, this reinforces my earlier point about the experienced teacher who is a novice mentor in a well established partnership scheme, where student teachers and HEI staff have high expectations of the quality of mentoring. A reflective mentor, however much a novice, will acknowledge this position, recognize its challenge and so face it with the right combination of novelty and uncertainty, seeking to build up a new and firm body of professional knowledge. This body of knowledge needs to grow rapidly in schools, as mentors now face the very considerable challenge of being the main assessors of student teachers' classroom competence. In the next chapter I shall focus on this area and so move on to considering the way newly qualified teachers can be supported in their first years in the profession.

5 Developing new English teachers: managing the transition into the profession

In the great majority of the book so far I have been attempting to help a mentor to review the demands of the role and to find ways of becoming a reflective mentor in the spirit of the reflective practitioner. I have tried to give some sense of the exciting scope, but also the challenging scale, of the mentor's role and of the demands that the role places on an individual and on an institution. In this chapter I shall begin by drawing together threads from the rest of the book and by examining the biggest single formal responsibility of a mentor: assessment. This discussion of the principles and practice of assessing student teachers leads, reasonably logically, into a consideration of how to assess and support beginning teachers of English. In particular, I wish to look at some approaches to helping teachers to learn about teaching that I feel can be used with almost any teachers, from the student to the highly experienced. I shall then move on to consider how departments can support beginning teachers, looking at 'daily life', meetings and training days. Finally, I shall review some of the issues related to appraisal and Ofsted.

The move to school-based assessment of student teachers

In Chapter 1, we reviewed the changes to teacher education that have led to the introduction of the school-based model and examined there some of the advantages and disadvantages of this model. One of the most significant shifts has been to giving schools the power to pass or fail students on their 'practical' competence. For some HEIs this was a very uncomfortable change: how can the HEI validate an award that, in a sense, it does not control? Uncomfortable or not, HEIs that wished to stay in initial teacher education have had to comply with this regulation. Inevitably, the way assessment is carried out can vary from one partnership scheme to another, but the framework is very fixed.

It is noteworthy that, at the time of writing, secondary schools in Northern Ireland simply rejected this style of partnership model and so assessment there has stayed entirely in the hands of HEIs. One of their principle objections was that they did not wish to have this *level* of responsibility for student teachers. However, student teachers in Northern Ireland will still have to spend 24 of their 36 weeks in school, so some new mode of assessment will almost certainly have to be developed.

I am not suggesting that schools generally have no experience of assessing student teachers, on the contrary, but I have certainly found that the idea of *having* to assess students and, ultimately, *very formally*, with a student teacher's future career resting on such a decision, has caused a number of problems and anxieties. At an impressionistic and personal level this change has been noticeable, to me, for the way it has tended to 'soften' school judgement. I have found that where a student is a clear 'failure', there has been remarkably unanimous agreement between all the partners. However, where a student has been 'borderline' or rather erratic, I have found schools decidedly leaning to the side of the student. A few years previously, I might have visited a school specifically to plead for a student to have more time or a fresh class or two to help her get through to 'passing the course'. Often, a department would be ready to fail the student, telling me that I should not let such a doubtful case get through. Usually, we negotiated some useful changes and it certainly made a positive difference sometimes, to some students. However, more recently I have visited schools and found myself saying that the 'difficult' student in question is taking up too much of their time, draining their energy and not responding to their advice, so perhaps they should at least declare the student a likely failure. At this stage, departments tend to argue for giving the student more time: what about a fresh class or two, and so on. It is partly that the 'boot is now on the other foot' and, significantly, that the student does *belong* in the department, having spent so much time there that the department properly feels very responsible for what happens. What I am emphasizing here is that the change in the assessment process can be felt in school and that we are developing ways to face the challenge of school-based assessment, but that the process is still being explored and refined. It is not clear yet whether this aspect of school-based teacher education is as much of a success as other elements.

Another aspect, related to assessment, of my time as an HEI tutor under the old HEI-based model was that I frequently felt that schools expected, in my view, rather too much of student teachers too quickly. Then the students tended to 'belong' to the HEI, and schools, I certainly felt, could be very hostile to students who caused problems or were finding it hard to come to terms with being properly professional. I had strong sympathy with both parties, having worked in schools for many years and as I was now working closely with student teachers on a daily basis. Neither 'party' was clear enough about the context of the other. This element of *expectation* is also now changing.

Gradually, but very definitely, partnership schemes are coming to a much more appropriately consensual view of what to expect from student (and beginning) teachers at different stages of their development. Overall, then, with the proper safeguards and establishment of equity between schools in partnership schemes, I welcome the move to giving schools the *major say* in the assessment of 'practical' competence, although safeguards do need to be built into the course structure. I do not think, however, that the changes have made the assessment of student teachers any 'easier'. It has made it more difficult but overall more accurate and more developmental for the schools involved. One of the main themes of this last third of the book will be how the partnership model of school-based teacher education provides a foundation for long-term change and professional development. Resolving the difficulties involved in the process of assessing student teachers, rigorously but fairly, and ensuring comparability across a range of very different contexts, is, in itself, valuable. During the course of some work on defining ability in English I tried to sum up that rather notorious idea by saying that it is not so much a 'Problematic concept as a valuably complicated concept' (Goodwyn, 1995: 9). What I was stressing there, and I feel is equally apposite here, is the importance of avoiding the temptation to over-simplify. Some processes are complicated and difficult because they take into account a multiple of variables yet seek to use an agreed framework for judgement; simplification could only lead to less accurate, and less fair, judgements.

Assessing teaching quality is difficult and complex and assessing someone learning to teach is likely to be more so, not less. I think that there was a clear expectation from the governmental architects of school-based teacher education that, once the power of assessment was wrested away from the 'theorists' in HEIs, much no-nonsense simplicity would follow. Teachers, the real, hard-nosed, toughened campaigners, would soon sort out entrants to the profession and get rid of any 'namby-pambies'. I know plenty of highly experienced English teachers, and they are certainly seasoned campaigners, but they refuse to operate simplistic models of student teacher assessment. They have also been very vocal about needing lots of support and guidance in this area and in wanting justice to be done through a series of external checks on their local judgements. By and large, such teachers have accepted that assessing student teaching is properly difficult and are keen to develop sophisticated ways of fair and rigorous assessment.

Coaching and assessing student teachers

The framework for school-based teacher education is fixed and was described, albeit briefly, in Chapter 1. The assessment model is a competency model and all partnership schemes, and also school-only schemes, must use it. This is not a book in which a whole range of assessment methodologies can be discussed, but it is essential for all reflective mentors to consider some of the advantages and disadvantages of the competency approach and to plan for the ways in which they will make use of competencies themselves and of other assessment techniques. It is useful to remember that the 'old' system was a mixed model and, although it varied from place to place, it tended to have some, or all, of these features:

- Students had to produce a series of formal assignments, set and marked by HEI tutors, some HEI, some school-focused.
- Students took 'theory' examinations, usually at the end of the course.
- Students were required to produce a record of lessons actually planned, taught and evaluated by the student (the teaching practice file).
- Each student was seen, and assessed, a number of times by an HEI tutor.
- Schools provided brief written evidence about a student's practical work (this had to be based on something and was usually a collective account of observations by several teachers over a period of time).
- Students often had to take a second subject, and carry out some teaching in that subject area, for which some, or all, of the above applied.
- Students were assessed on a scale and were usually awarded grades of some kind. These tended to be composite grades reflecting a practical aspect and a separate, 'theoretical', aspect. These grades might or might not be communicated to the actual student.

In the decade leading up to the change to school-based teacher education, many of these practices were changing, and terminal examinations and student grading had virtually disappeared in England and Wales by the beginning of the 1990s. However, many of the above features *remain in place*, and they do so after careful negotiation between partners, including of course schools. The competence model has not therefore removed what might usefully be called the familiar evidence base for our assessments.

However, a competence approach can seem very impersonal, abstract and fragmented when first encountered. It can seem very distant from the holistic nature of the *experience* of skilful teaching. The teachers I have worked with, in a number of subject disciplines, have found the competencies extremely valuable, *but not at first*. I feel it is important, through the discussion of two examples, to show some of the apparent awkwardness of competencies but also how, if properly handled and thoroughly discussed, they can provide an excellent and generally fair means of student assessment.

One last step before we begin this process is to focus succinctly on what it is that we all are trying to assess. The simplistic models that I have referred to earlier in the book would have a fairly crude premise, something like: 'If they can teach, then a teacher simply needs to watch them teaching, often enough, to be able to say that they can do it.' However, the teachers that I know are very unhappy with anything as simplistic as this, because, as they know extremely well, it does not begin to address the complexities of teaching and the constant adjustments that teachers need to make to ensure good learning. It also, very obviously, leaves out all the myriad things that happen outside the classroom that make sure that good learning take place inside it. Highly accomplished teachers carry so much around in their heads that the evidence of their thinking and reflection is usually invisible. Partnership models are universally concerned to help students to generate sufficient explicit evidence of their competence for it to be visible to all concerned parties.

I would suggest that HEI tutors and school mentors would want to see evidence of a whole range of activities in order both to assess a student's progress and to diagnose where a student most needs help. The partnership model that I work with uses the following four major headings. They have been regularly reviewed and all the partners have subscribed to them.

- *Area 1.* Students should acquire knowledge and understanding of factors relating to whole-school issues, systems and practices, and should demonstrate competence in the wide range of activities expected of teachers in the whole-school context. In doing so, they should draw on theoretical models and practical insights as appropriate.
- *Area 2.* Students should acquire knowledge and understanding of factors relating to classroom practice and should demonstrate competence in the wide range of activities expected of teachers in the context of the subject classroom. In doing so, they should draw on theoretical models and practical insights as appropriate.
- *Area 3.* Students should recognize that the model for student teacher learning provides a mechanism for long-term professional development and should demonstrate that they are taking first steps towards such development.
- *Area 4.* Students should define some personal goals related to whole-school issues and subject teaching. Some will be addressed during the course, others may be intended as a focus for longer-term professional development.

The first three areas are each followed by the phrase, 'To demonstrate competence in this area students must consistently . . .', and the phrase is followed by a number of specific competence statements: area 1 has 11, area 2 has 31 and area 3 has seven; area 4 is treated as a single competence. Area 2 is the 'practical' area and covers the ground that the mentor must scrutinize. I include this level of detail to demonstrate the care and the proper attention to sophisticated assessment that is becoming the normal pattern in partnership courses. These are the key focal points of assessment and they help to illuminate where evidence is needed; evidence that the student teachers must either produce themselves or have produced about them.

The two examples that I am going to discuss, briefly, both come from area 2, the area that is the mentor's chief concern. The idea that there are 29 other competencies may seem rather off-putting, but they are in fact mostly remarkable for being straightforward and entirely uncontroversial. For example, a statement such as 'Have knowledge and understanding of the National Curriculum in their subject and of the framework of statutory requirements' is hardly likely to confuse anyone, and its relevance is absolutely clear. I think the relevance and clarity of 'understand and demonstrate the notions of continuity and progression in their subject' is the same. However, certainly in English, 'continuity and progression' are problematic concepts. They are problematic because most English teachers, operating a mainly personal growth model, are interested in long-term, recursive development; there are very few quick results in English, and when they do happen, they tend to be in individual pupils. Not only is progression tricky to demonstrate but it is an area dogged by disagreement and political interference. The levels in the National Curriculum for English have generated much debate and heat, but little professional warmth towards them.

A student teacher needs particular help with a competence like this and a mentor may need, as is usual in planned learning, to help in stages. There would be little point in assessing such a competence until relatively late in students' time in school: they would not have taught for long enough to have witnessed much continuity or progression. However, a student needs to consider and try to understand this tricky concept once they are in school and can study the teaching of others. For a student teacher, understanding how a lesson fits into a sequence is rather like a photographic negative developing extremely slowly: it takes a long time for a clear picture to emerge, but once it does, the concept is clear too. With this crucial aspect of teaching, the competence statement can act as an excellent diagnostic element in a *developing conversation*. The reflective mentor can start discussions when the student is observing others, including the mentor's own teaching, building up the student teacher's understanding. Later the mentor and the HEI tutor can prompt the student to think systematically about this point as she plans and evaluates. Finally, it is a fair and highly valuable question to put back to the student, 'Where is the evidence of consistently appropriate attention to continuity and progression in your teaching?' At this point a competent student will be able to demonstrate this attention; her evidence can include her file, her notes and observations, the written feedback she has received from others and so on. It is very important to note that much of this evidence is inevitably in written form as a record. I would suggest that written evidence is valuable not just as a kind of hard copy, but also as a highly developmental activity in itself. Producing written evidence of your competence requires reflection and evaluation and then the considered articulation of your position.

My second example, 'recognize the importance of natural justice, dignity and equality and strive towards motivating and empowering pupils,' raises a different issue about the mentor's role in assessment. Some student teachers and mentors have found the wording of this competence somewhat problematic at first. After initial discussions they are tempted to simplify it to just 'being fair' but, usually after further discussions, they wish to retain it, as it is, because its more elaborate wording is also much more demanding and powerful. Here, I feel, the competence in question makes a serious and even profound demand on a student teacher. Perhaps readers will initially feel that this is a contradiction of my emphasis throughout this book that students should not be overloaded and that mentors need constantly to evaluate how much students can usefully cope with. I would argue, consistently I hope, that school-based teacher education can make properly powerful intellectual and personal demands on student teachers. These entrants to the profession should profoundly question the educational status quo and they should try out their own values in relation to children. Words like 'justice', 'dignity', 'equality' and 'empowering' are not educational jargon. They are concerned with the *essential purposes of education*, they are about absolute principles. They may not sit well with many of the cynically narrow pressures on schools to compete with each other and to spend their budgets on marketing themselves, but they represent the heart of truly good teaching.

A 'competence' can sound as dull and neutral as 'can park a car'; as it happens, parking a car is a necessary and useful skill and can be a difficult one to manage. Only in very rare circumstances might it be viewed as an action imbued with natural justice. Teaching, and especially good teaching, is neither dull nor 'neutral'. For the children it is stimulating, demanding and genuinely challenging. It is an activity imbued, through and through, with natural justice. Good teaching fosters learning that is unquestionably 'empowering', and every reader of this book is likely to have many vivid memories of leaving lessons with what we often call 'that buzz', that joyful feeling that what we tried went really well and that the children have had a genuine learning experience. I would argue strongly that these moments are filled with professional satisfaction because we feel that the whole group has been involved and *collectively* challenged. Such experiences tend to be rather special for several reasons, but one key aspect would be that justice was there, its presence felt, because the irritations and dissatisfactions of injustice and unfairness are markedly absent. Returning to the competence itself, its rather elaborate wording is itself a real challenge. It needs thinking about and reflecting upon and it is hard to achieve consistently. Of course, a mentor knows this and can ask for the right kind of consistency from a student teacher, but there is no need to diminish or play down the properly high demands that this competence makes. Looked at in this way, I hope I have made a case for this complex competence being a very good one because of what it demands of the student and the mentor.

The strength of the current use of competencies in partnership teacher education is that it has far surpassed the somewhat secretive approaches of the past. Every evaluation of the competence assessment model that I have undertaken with mentors in English has produced a consistency of response which can be summed up as:

- Competencies initially look off-putting and can sound difficult.
- They need discussion and contextualization.

- The student, the mentor and the HEI tutor (and other involved professionals) need to revisit them to maintain an agreed position.
- They are extremely productive for promoting discussion and reflection in all the involved individuals.
- They provide an excellent common focus between all members of the partnership team (my estimate for my course is that this is at least 1000 people per year).
- They provide a fair and rigorous means of diagnostic and summative assessment that can be moderated across a wide range of contexts.
- Their level of detail helps everyone to be systematic and to record evidence systematically.
- They are always being read in a fresh way and therefore challenged by new participants, such as the students, new school members of the partnership and external examiners; they are then subject to revision and improvement.

The unanimity of support for the model has been very striking, but I am aware that some readers may well have had more variable experiences.

For all mentors, regardless of potential dissatisfactions with current practice, the essential points are that discussions about progress need to be open and clear. Some kind of criteria to refer to and return to are absolutely necessary. The mentor is, in this way, always *coaching* the student teacher towards an understood goal. The aim for all concerned is to help the student through, not to catch her out. The mentor is, rather like a coach in the sporting sense, always looking to help the student get better, and so discusses with the student her progress and the places where improvements can be made. The mentor has a role that is not only formally powerful, as chief assessor, but equally intellectually powerful, consistently helping students to think through their developing approaches to teaching.

Finding a means to reflection

We all benefit enormously from help with learning. Teachers dedicate their working lives with children to this idea. English teachers draw chiefly on language and literature as their major resources for pupils' learning. I do not need to convince English teachers that stories are powerful in themselves and powerful aids to learning; one thing they help us to do especially well is to reflect upon humanity in general, and our own humanity as an individual in particular. English teachers become highly expert at choosing texts that will engage and stimulate children, and even better at finding successful ways of approaching such texts in order to motivate that engagement and stimulation. There is a useful element of consistency and predictability in this developed expertise with texts. One thing that makes English such an enjoyable subject to teach, however, is the remarkable power of children to interpret stories and to offer different ideas about meanings; what we have, then, is predictable unpredictability. That stimulating sense of novelty and uncertainty we examined earlier in relation to teaching generally is normally and very enjoyably present in many English lessons. Using 'stories' to help students (and teachers) to learn to teach should appeal particularly to English mentors, and there is an increasing body of professional knowledge to support this idea.[1]

I am going to devote several pages to discussing this approach and to offering some examples that I have found particularly useful. My examples are just that, my examples, and readers will very likely have much more effective ones for their own use. The main purpose here is to help mentors of English students to think about how to draw on their own very extensive experience in a systematic and reflective way, selecting some experiences that offer students learning opportunities. I would also argue that these stories become part of a professional repertoire that is of potential value to a range of colleagues, the most obvious beneficiaries, as well as student teachers, being beginning teachers of English. The following pages are intended to be of use in themselves for work with student teachers but also to act as a bridge into thinking about the ongoing professional needs of newly qualified teachers (NQTs).

The method that I am going to describe is one very close to that frequently used by English teachers using, consciously or not, reader response theory (Rosenblatt, 1978). Reader response theory positions readers as active meaning makers who bring all their own experience to play in trying to interpret a text. It considers that readers begin with tentative and uncertain readings and, through a series of attempted interpretations, move to an interpretation that is satisfactory for the reader at that time. This theory therefore both validates and values the openness of interpretations and offers lots of scope for reviewing one's position and formulating another 'satisfactory' position. It also validates the idea that an interpretation is intimately and properly connected to one's repertoire of personal experience and that such experience inevitably, and usefully, changes our position in relation to texts.

I offer this rather potted version of reader response to help readers to make comparisons between their use of texts and the use I am about to describe. What I might call 'teacher response theory' is remarkably close to reader response theory and draws on exactly the same principle of active meaning making. An example will, I hope, illustrate this point.

I have argued very strongly that mentors need to learn about the positions that student teachers occupy during the course, but especially early on, because their position may be mostly unconscious and possibly problematic; they need help articulating that position. It is vital for a mentor to 'get a look' at her mentee's subject position as a starting point. As I pointed out in Chapter 2, student teachers are usually keen to impress those in positions of expertise that they 'know nothing', putting forward the illusion that they have no position as yet, and that the expert, on the contrary, knows everything. I hope I have demonstrated that this is not a useful perspective for either 'expert' or 'novice' and certainly is not productive of genuine dialogue between the partners.

A mentor needs to help a student to recognize her position and use it as a starting point for learning. Consider the following example about teaching poetry:

> The class teacher has asked you to develop a unit of work on poetry for her year 9 middle ability group. The group has done some poetry lower down the school, but this unit is meant to be their first, intensive look at poetry and is expected to prepare them for poetry work at GCSE. You have been given carte blanche and can use whatever poetry and whatever approach you like. The class teacher has intimated that you are doing poetry because she is never very comfortable with it and does not really expect pupils to like poetry.
>
> One of your main concerns is the first, introductory double lesson. Three colleagues have independently given you very different advice. One has suggested that year 9 is the time to get pupils to take poetry seriously. You should concentrate on an important writer and make sure that, by the end of the lesson, the class has come to recognize just how complex and rich a serious poem can be. Another colleague suggests that you deliberately approach poetry as ordinary, as a part of everyday life, that you should begin with song lyrics, posters, advertising jingles and so on, getting pupils to recognize their own encounters with poetry. Finally, one teacher has suggested that you get pupils to write some poetry in a variety of ways, perhaps for several lessons; then you should move on to looking at published poetry. Which approach do you believe would be most effective?

I hope that readers feel that this 'situation' fits with their own experiences of English teachers but, as I mentioned above, you may feel immediately that you have more accurate or more pertinent examples. Initially I would ask students to study the example closely and to find (as with reader response theory) their own, tentative position, in other words what approach they might take, then to discuss with others why they feel that a particular approach, or combination of approaches, is the one they would choose. We might then discuss as a group the pros and cons of the various approaches, giving individuals a chance to return to their tentative position and to see if they have come to a satisfactory position. A useful question at this stage is to ask them to reflect on the fact that they seem to 'know' rather a lot, that they are already making key, professional choices and that this is a good thing to do. It is also helpful in terms of professional contextualization, because these choices are real and there really is no one right way. To return to reader response theory, we are looking at how we make predictions (as readers) and so try to draw on all our textual and personal knowledge. In 'teacher response theory' terms student teachers are drawing on their teaching knowledge and their personal knowledge; they are being active meaning makers. This particular example about poetry can be returned to on more than one occasion. A particularly appropriate moment later might be when there is a need to consider the teaching of poetry itself. Using our earlier focus on the counselling model that expects the mentor to adopt a positive and accepting stance, such materials are especially useful because they begin with a concrete example of teaching but not one that 'belongs' to either partner in the conversation.

For a student teacher the constant, and understandable, concern is about classroom management, basic discipline. A great difficulty for anyone in a mentoring position is to help student teachers to see that management includes everything from the choice of poem to the tone of voice that they use to introduce it, to the way the seats are organized and so on. It is not a 'simple matter' of discipline. However, students have a very strong need to feel that they are focusing on classroom management and, as Maslow (see Chapter 4), helpfully reminds us, unless we answer basic needs, higher level ones will not seem important or worthwhile. Here is an example of a classroom moment that helps students to feel that they are focusing on classroom management with particular reference to discipline.

Maria is teaching a difficult year 10 class. The lesson is about the language of persuasion, using advertisements as the examples. It is the first lesson of the day (always the best one of the week for this group), the pupils have been looking at advertisements for houses and flats and identifying the kinds of language that are used, and they have had one try at writing an example of their own. It is now two-thirds of the way through the lesson and the class are chatting and working. Maria is helping a pair at the front when Wayne, who always sits at the back, calls out 'Hey, stop that. Miss, Miss, she keeps turning round Miss and interfering with my work, she's bullying me!' Wayne grins and looks around the class, his tone is jokey. Sharon denies she has looked around and the class looks up for a moment to see Maria's reaction. She walks slowly over to the two pupils and speaks quietly to them. The class returns to work.

Maria returns to the front of the class and is about to speak when the two pupils erupt again in a loud fuss. Maria, clearly irritated, says loudly, 'That's quite enough now. You will have to move.' Wayne says 'Who miss?' Maria hesitates and says 'Sharon, you had better move and work over there.' She points. 'Come on now.' Sharon pleads, 'Why should I have to move, Miss?' Maria says loudly, 'Come on now, I said move.' The whole class is now watching. Sharon puts her head down and starts to write busily. Maria stands irresolutely at the front, the class returns to work and chatter. Sharon keeps her head down and writes on.

After a minute Maria says, 'Right everyone, can I have your attention,' and proceeds to talk about the next activity. Ten minutes later the lesson ends. Sharon leaves quietly without speaking to or being spoken to by Maria.

The first thing to comment on is that student teachers have just as strong a 'position' on discipline as they do on the subject of English. In fact, because of their insecurities they usually have even stronger views on 'good discipline' than they do on teaching English. Readers will be very familiar with the fact that almost everyone in the universe has a strong position on discipline and on how teachers should 'enforce it', however unqualified and inexperienced they are. It is no wonder that students, who are desperately concerned to understand 'discipline', have strong views. As discussed above, they begin as *unconsciously incompetent* and they need to travel some distance before they become even *consciously incompetent*.

Their unconscious incompetence does not mean that they have nothing to say about this example. In fact they have volumes to say and this little anecdote has occupied quite a few productive hours. However, very like with a narrative text, I would argue that one of the very first acts is to help students step back from judgemental comments (of which they will offer many such: 'Well, *obviously* she should have . . .') and simply to establish a tentative account of the 'incident'. In other words, what is the story?

A useful point to add here is that video footage of lessons, however hard to obtain, is very rich material for discussions about teaching. However, students are initially no more skilled in commenting on video footage than they are on direct personal observation. The great advantage of video footage, to state the obvious but important, is that it can be viewed several times and treated rather like a text; this allows for the richness of interpretation that reader response theory is fundamentally concerned with. This element of successive interpretations allows the initial attempts to be tentative and, I would strongly argue, this is extremely helpful in helping student teachers to employ some reflection before being tempted to make superficial judgements. Written scenarios, as with our two examples so far, also have the advantage that they can be used to foster rich interpretations.

However, student teachers seem to need quite firm direction in simply reaching an account of a lesson. The question 'What actually happened?' causes immense problems; student teachers can be far more concerned, initially at least, to criticize than to understand. HEI tutors and mentors want them to be far more understanding and then appropriately critical.

To return to the written example, student teachers can be helped first to reach an account of 'what happened'. This can actually take time, as they distinguish between events and comments. I find a productive next stage is to ask for some views on the key moment when they feel that something went 'wrong'. What was the 'critical incident'? This use of selective attention seems to help with providing an appropriate focus and with helping them to see that others will view apparently 'transparent' incidents in a way that colours them differently, leading to different interpretations and so to the recommendation of alternative strategies.

Part of the discussion of this story invites 'What would have happened if . . . ?' Students can explore the real alternatives available in a clearly contextualized situation. This, in itself, is very valuable again in making them accept (eventually) that there is no one right way. Equally, it helps with developing an evaluative approach which is less judgemental and more about understanding the situation, more concerned with recognizing key factors and much less with 'blaming', which tends to lead to simplistic judgements and, certainly in my view, less thoughtful analysis. Students can be encouraged to talk around the whole context of this incident and to explore issues about classroom relationships, about authority and natural justice, about the pastoral system and school sanctions and so on. A useful concluding focus can be asking them to consider what should happen between now and the next lesson, and also how that lesson might be introduced.

I feel that this incident does generate rich interpretations that are a genuine aid to reflection. It also offers scope for one other dimension that is of particular value to student teachers, and that is the crucial issue of how to talk about classroom difficulties. One approach is to point out to them that 'I was really there, this is an incident that I witnessed and so I needed to discuss the lesson afterwards with the student.' What do the students think would be a fair and useful approach to this conversation? How does the mentor think the student teacher is feeling? How would she be feeling? My aim here is to begin the process of sensitizing mentors to the whole issue of 'advice', because advice does need to be honest and clear. In the end a mentor is a crucial assessor, but does advice need to be harsh and strident? To extend this point about advice and dialogue, I shall offer here a final example from my classroom 'repertoire', again based on a real experience and again raising a number of issues about English teaching.

It is the last, double lesson of the afternoon and Sheila, a student teacher, three weeks into her main teaching practice, is about to start some new work with her mixed ability, year 8 group. She also has the group first thing on Monday for a double lesson, and late on Thursday morning for a single lesson. The school is a mixed, medium-sized comprehensive. However, because of local rumours that it might close, the school has not really attracted a balanced intake for several years. As a result, all classes tend to have more average or below average pupils than in a genuine comprehensive. This class has 16 boys and 11 girls.

Sheila has struggled with this class so far and she hopes to establish a better atmosphere with a unit on fairy stories. She has chosen it because she feels that all pupils have an understanding of such stories and so they should be able to contribute. She expects to look at a range of stories and then to encourage the class, the following week, to write modern fairy stories of their own. She has prepared some handouts, which include an A4 sheet containing several short, differing versions of 'Little Red Riding Hood' and a chart on which pupils can write story titles and then analyse them by identifying some key characteristics of each story. The class are seated in a horseshoe pattern with a central block of tables in the middle. Only girls sit on this table. Boys range around the room, with one especially difficult group in the far corner. The class enter noisily and take some time to quieten down. There is still considerable background noise but Sheila begins: 'I am sure that you all like fairy stories and so we are going to start a big, new unit of work on fairy stories.' Loud groans from the boys. 'Now, come on, everyone knows some fairy stories from when they were little.' There is considerable noise and several boys are calling out to each other, 'Who can give me an example of a fairy story?' There is general noise and no response. 'Come on now.'

A girl near the front says quietly 'Red Riding Hood'. 'Yes, that's it, any more suggestions?' She looks up around the class. Almost all the boys are talking to each other and paying no attention to her.

There are many things 'wrong' with this lesson and, as I have said, students rush headlong into the judgemental; they are properly *unconscious*, especially early in the course, of the similar, and entirely normal, mistakes that they too will make. Many of the questions outlined above are appropriate for discussing and analysing this classroom episode, and it produces a great deal of useful reflection, especially here as the student teacher's approach contains such a range of missed opportunities.

This episode is especially useful for helping students to think about *how advice needs to be focused*. Mentors can produce a very long list of 'things to do' for the student teacher here and, once it is pointed out that she might be on the receiving end of such an impossible looking agenda, she is prepared to reflect on the basic idea of selective attention. Which one, or perhaps two, things from the list would be worth detailed discussion and follow-up on the next occasion? Once a point was agreed, how would an observer monitor it and offer feedback? I am not suggesting for a moment, unfortunately, that these activities change student teachers' behaviours in a dramatic way. However, the 'stories' are based on authentic classroom episodes, they have a genuine 'feel' of reality (students especially value this element) and they produce well focused and reflective discussions that do not mask the complexities of teaching. They offer an insight into the teacher's need for a knowledge of alternative strategies and of 'reflection in action'. They also provide and stimulate, as does literature, a place where 'readers' of all levels can share their expertise and develop meanings. For the mentor, very like the English teacher working with children on a story, the nature of the insights and meanings produced helps the mentor to see how a student is coming along, and provides useful access to some of their thinking.

From student teacher to newly qualified teacher

As I have emphasized already, these classroom episodes are very useful for a number of purposes and can certainly engage highly experienced, as well as student, teachers. They are extremely useful for working with beginning teachers and this leads us on to some issues relating to NQTs and to the extended role of the mentor. The majority of the book concerns the need for a mentor for student teachers who are operating in a school-based system. This is enough of a new role to be a really important professional challenge for the teachers involved, their departments and their schools. It might now be argued that student teachers who have been through this system ought to start their careers on a very firm footing, perhaps needing less support in their first years of teaching. The abolition of the probationary year seemed to suggest that a PGCE, or its equivalent, was quite sufficient for most beginning teachers. However, it was the then DES that abolished the probationary year and the profession generally was unhappy with this move.

Since that rather negative change, there has been some attention to the professional development of beginning teachers. The term 'induction' is now relatively familiar and most schools operate a programme for NQTs, run usually by a senior member of staff, that is designed to provide a coordinated introduction to the school and to provide regular opportunities for NQTs to meet and to discuss their development and their concerns. So does this mean that newly qualified English teachers, especially if they have had a successful year in a school-based PGCE, are sufficiently supported? I think the answer must be that they are, at least, recognized as needing support and that they are receiving some which has formal status, but any profession dedicated to learning surely ought to model lifelong learning in all its work.

Fortunately, most PGCE courses expect their students to formulate some goals for early professional development and to arrive in schools in September with some thought through priorities. This mechanism, embedded within initial teacher education, articulates well with the formal expectations of induction and with the growing emphases on appraisal and inspection. However, there is a great deal more that can happen through the active intervention of a departmental mentor.

The concept of workplace mentors is a very traditional one, but it has become radically energized by different ideas about management and about creating 'learning organizations' (Caldwell and Carter, 1993). These ideas focus on giving a novice access to the knowledge she needs, when she needs it, through ensuring that a mentor is close at hand for easy contact. It is worth stating at this point that someone who is a mentor for student teachers may well be ideally suited to mentor other 'novices', but may be fully stretched by the demands of that role; to my knowledge there is currently no actual provision for workplace mentoring for teachers. This lack of provision may well mean that schools are forced to give workplace mentoring relatively low status and to provide no resources. What I am outlining below tries to take account of this lack of resources, while recognizing that 'goodwill' is not inexhaustible.

The basic situation of an NQT provides a useful starting point for anyone planning to support her. The great majority of NQTs of English will be products of a school-based, partnership PGCE course. If so, then they will have completed some kind of profile at the conclusion of the course and, as mentioned above, they will have reflected on their initial needs. A departmental mentor has an excellent starting point in something that introduces NQTs, gives insights into their developing subject 'position' and offers some goals for discussion and, later, for review. Should the NQT have no profile, for whatever reason, there would be much to be gained by inviting her to produce one. Finally, the mentor knows the new context and is likely to have a reasonable understanding of the realistic, or not, nature of the NQT's goals in this new context, especially given the demands of the first year of full-time teaching. It is my experience that student teachers, at the end of the PGCE course, will say, 'You said it would be exhausting but I would not have believed that it could be so hard.' If I see them a year later, after their first year of full-time teaching, they say, 'You said it would be exhausting and harder than the PGCE but I would never have believed it could be this hard.' There are few things so demanding as the first year of teaching. Already, then, a mentor may need to adjust any NQT's goals and targets to make them manageable and realistic, especially when they are reviewed over the year.

This idea of review is crucial. The one thing NQTs do have is qualified status: they are 'real' teachers. The irony of this 'real' status is to discover that, although student teachers may now be 'below' them, they at least have a reasonable amount of attention. NQTs may soon find that a full timetable, a pastoral responsibility and a full National Curriculum administration load stretch them to breaking point, with very little attention centred on them at any time. A review meeting may not solve many of these problems but it gives status to NQTs and a high profile to their needs and goals. Once more we can refer to Maslow's point about helping people to belong and therefore to want to contribute. If NQTs' basic needs are being at least acknowledged they are much more likely to become valuable department members.

One basic need is *recognition*. NQTs may find not only that they receive very little attention but that suddenly they are back to being consciously incompetent. Whereas, at the end of their course, they were often being congratulated and praised, now they hear only the voice of their own self-criticisms after what feel like 'failing' lessons. I am not suggesting that teachers do not talk to each other and that NQTs are somehow ostracized and abandoned, but it is important to recognize that insecurity makes people defensive and anxious. It is much easier for someone who is feeling defensive to 'pretend' to cope than to admit, openly, that she is not coping. We examined this issue earlier in relation to student teachers and I commented, as an example, on my own failures to use the support around me in my first years of teaching. NQTs, as a result of their school-based courses, should be more open and more prepared to seek support, but the provision of a mentor helps this process enormously.

The idea of review is vital because of the status it gives to the meeting, but it is equally important because it should be two-way. Given that there are not likely to be resources for departmental mentors, they need support too. A review with the NQT is also about negotiating what a mentor can effectively contribute. Perhaps the mentor had planned to come and observe the NQT with a problematic class but is finding it impossible to come because of losing 'free' periods to cover and through the pressures of normal work. Such typical pressures need describing and discussing so that a review is not a token meeting but a genuine one for evaluating progress and planning development, taking into account changing contextual demands.

So what can a departmental mentor do, apart from being a good listener and offering pertinent advice? The following list offers a range of suggestions, some very similar to those ideas set out earlier for student teachers but some very different:

- offer praise and support;
- observe and (when appropriate) critique lessons;
- help to plan and prepare lessons;
- teach parallel lessons (e.g. same year group, approximately the same content) to compare and discuss outcomes;
- swap classes to provide points of comparison and contrast;
- discuss and review schemes of work;
- focus on individual pupils and help to devise strategies for working with them;
- be observed by the NQT and then discuss the lessons;
- provide observation opportunities with other staff;
- negotiate and define departmental tasks (e.g. evaluating and selecting resources, helping with administration, liaising with other departments, attending meetings);
- discuss and select in-service courses;
- recommend resources and 'background' reading;
- discuss case studies and teaching scenarios;
- identify department and school-wide expertise ('You should talk to so and so about role play');
- connect the NQT to other support, such as the local education authority, the National Association for the Teaching of English (NATE) or the United Kingdom Reading Association (UKRA), all of which may have local activities;
- connect the NQT to teachers in other local schools;
- differentiate between short-term and long-term goals.

This list should provide enough scope for a departmental mentor to select apposite and timely activities and to keep some novel and refreshing challenges available for the NQT and the mentor. It should also provide enough scope for genuine negotiation, giving the NQT a feeling of some control and direction over the support programme. Such a programme might well be planned for two years, rather than one, helping NQTs to see that they will continue to have support and challenge over a longer period of time. It also gives the mentor the opportunity to adjust the programme, depending on the NQTs development and the changing context. Should the mentor leave or have to turn attention elsewhere, then the agreed programme helps the replacement mentor to review progress and to inherit a thoughtfully negotiated scheme.

Appraisal

Appraisal is now a fairly common, even routine, activity in many schools. Readers may therefore feel familiar with it, even rather tired of it, but for others it may be untried and, perhaps, still rather threatening. It is worth stating first that the teaching profession was somewhat out of step with many other professions and certainly with the commercial world, where appraisal was not only a regular and integrated activity but a powerful and meaningful one. At the simplest level, promotion often depended upon it. Equally, the 'industrial' model of appraisal, certainly where it was successful, was a two-way process. If the appraiser wished to suggest shortcomings in the appraisee's performance then the appraisee could point out where there may have been inadequate training or lack of available resources; this identification of the problem might lead to the action for the future to be for the employer to fill those gaps, allowing for reappraisal at a suitable later date. This description offers a very benign view of appraisal but also one that fits in with all the research quoted throughout this book about *engaging individuals' motivation*. We know that fear, as in fear of losing one's job, is a powerful motivator, but it is not inspirational and neither does it promote collective effort. It keeps people low down in their hierarchy of needs, and thus does not promote genuine involvement or commitment.

The teaching profession is still experimenting with appraisal and it is by no means either firmly established or, as yet, generally respected. I am outlining, very briefly, some simple points about the purpose and format for appraisal so that mentors can bear these in mind in their own work. The chief purpose of appraisal should be to help the appraisee to review her achievements and focus on how she can consolidate achievement and improve in the future. Part of this process may well involve examining problems and weaknesses and identifying the nature of such things and their origins. However, appraisal is utterly counter-productive unless the appraisee trusts the criteria being used. A second purpose of appraisal is to review how the individual is working within the various contexts of the institution: department, pastoral team, whole school and so on. These two main purposes require that the format for appraisal is fit for the purpose. Both parties need to prepare for the actual meeting (or meetings), providing some written material that has been agreed as the basis for the meeting and giving time to the meeting in a place that provides a suitably relaxed and confidential atmosphere. I expect that these points are obvious, but readers will know well that the ordinary, hectic nature of most schools frequently militates against providing even these basic elements. In the brief following section, given the difficulties described above, I aim simply to offer some perspectives on appraisal in relation to a mentor's role both with student teachers and with departmental colleagues, and on how mentors might make use of the appraisal of their mentees.

One of the chief purposes of this book is to help mentors to analyse and make the most of the role of mentor. It follows very logically, then, that when they are to be appraised by their school, this role should feature on the agenda. However, it may be the case that the appraiser either knows less than the appraisee about mentoring or has a rather outdated notion of how student teachers can be helped to learn. Even if the appraiser is more knowledgeable and more enlightened than this, it seems to me that there is a particular need for the mentor to provide some overview of her role. I appreciate that the appraisal will properly give only a proportion of time to mentoring, but I am arguing that it needs to be given a particular emphasis because the appraiser might, for whatever reason, see it as outside her brief, even as an HEI, rather than a school, matter.

I suggest that mentors provide a brief and pertinent account of their role, with some attention given to each of the following:

- an estimate of the time they have given to the role;
- a review of the support that they have received from school and from the relevant HEI (or possibly HEIs);
- some account of their management of the role's demands;
- a recommendation about ways forward, perhaps with the resource implications spelt out (for example, attendance at in-service courses);
- some comment on their evaluation of the role as part of their professional development.

These points should help both to inform the appraiser and to provide a context for discussion. Schools in general, but especially those committed to long-term partnerships, will need to build a consideration of mentorship into their own school development plans; appraisal is a useful mechanism for evaluating the impact of school-based teacher education and for identifying successful approaches to mentoring.

Many of the above points apply to a departmental mentor, especially as this tends to be an unresourced commitment, and it is even more important that the efficacy of the role is reviewed and evaluated. One essential difference here is that the appraisee has a chance to talk in confidence about the personal demands of the role. The departmental mentor may have found the role satisfying and valuable, in which case this success can be recorded and considered. However, the role may have been difficult because of the mentee, and the mentor may wish to explain this point, in properly professional confidence, often to someone outside her department. It may well be appropriate, therefore, for the appraiser to appraise both mentor and mentee in order for some professional objectivity to be established; such coordination may lie outside the scope of departmental mentors, but there is no reason why they should not put forward suggestions about such coordination that help to promote thoughtful professional development.

The final consideration is what use the departmental mentor can make of her own mentee's appraisal. First, it is worth considering that an NQT may already be receiving a range of valuable feedback during her first year, of which an appraisal is a key element, and so the mentor is playing a significant part in that supportive community and will naturally draw on the appraisal. However, if the NQT's experience is different, and she has had perhaps random and episodic feedback, then the mentor is perhaps as close as she will get to some form of appraisal. Should this be the context, then the mentor might consider providing one special meeting, late in the school year, that adopts the purpose and format of an appraisal (see above). My own view would be that such an 'informal' appraisal should only be undertaken if the mentee is clearly keen to be a leading part of it; the mentor might ask the NQT to consider what the value of such an occasion would be, given that she has had regular feedback and developmental discussions with the mentor. I am encouraging the mentor to place the mentee in *a leading role*, not because the mentees 'know the answers' but because they need to prioritize their questions.

However, for most departmental mentors, the situation is likely to be that they are in a position to draw on the mentee's appraisal in some way. There is the issue, touched on above, that appraisals are confidential occasions and that the mentor will probably have been the subject of part of that confidential discussion. The mentor can still draw very valuably on the appraisal discussion and some of the following points may help to focus the mentor–mentee follow-up conversation:

- The NQT might, first, simply 'describe' the appraisal process.
- What were the feelings of the NQT at the end of the appraisal?
- What relevance does the NQT feel that the appraisal has for her relationship with the mentor?
- What individual points have emerged from the appraisal that affect the NQT's plans for the future?
- What can the mentor do, if anything, to support the outcomes of the appraisal?

- Does the NQT want a response from the mentor about the outcomes of the appraisal?

The reader will note that, as with much of the general approach of the book, the mentor is holding back until the mentee reaches a position from which she can *invite* comment and advice.

Finally, the purpose of any of these appraisals is to contribute to the development of the individual and of the institution; it is part of an ongoing process. Nevertheless, and quite normally in human terms, it provides a particular focus at a particular time which can be extremely helpful in reviewing that ongoing process and in monitoring actual progress. At all the levels described above, the appraisal provides evidence that can be reviewed at subsequent appraisals and mentors should integrate this point into their own professional development and that of their mentees.

Other professional contributions, such as local education authorities and Ofsted

The past few years have witnessed a very distinct change in the nature of the external advice and criticism 'available' to schools on a regular basis. It is important to take a brief look at these changes because they once again place rather more weight on schools themselves and also because they have direct implications for partnership schools. The great majority of schools, until the early 1990s, had some kind of relationship with their local authority that meant that many 'critical friends' were available, to some extent 'on demand'. This advice came in the shape of local authority advisers, both subject specialists and individuals undertaking a more general role; the advice was 'already paid for' as a part of the LEA system. Schools were inspected, infrequently, by HMI, and although this was a challenging and rigorous business in itself, it did not involve the public machinery and vast amounts of paperwork that seem to be a regular feature of the current privatized model of inspection. A side-effect of current inspection procedures is that many schools now spend their money on 'pre-Ofsted' checks and on having their staff briefed on 'how to succeed in inspections'. There are many other features of these kinds of changes that affect schools – for example, grant maintained status, school financial management, the increased powers of governors and so on – and all have some direct relevance to mentorship.

I shall focus initially on the destabilizing and downgrading of the local education authority. For student teachers this has little direct impact on them. In a good partnership scheme they are reasonably well supported by the school and by another 'critical friend', the HEI, and I shall return to student teachers when looking at inspection. For an NQT, the LEA is a crucial element in her induction. Some LEAs continue to find money for induction programmes and to provide advisory teachers, part of whose brief is to support

NQTs, particularly those who are struggling in their first two years of full-time teaching. This is an excellent feature of the LEAs' work and long may it continue to exist. However, in places where it has withered away, the school has to provide induction and the departmental mentor's role takes on yet another level of challenge. Earlier in this chapter we listed a range of approaches that a departmental mentor might adopt, and this included to:

- discuss and select in-service courses;
- identify department and school-wide expertise ('You should talk to so and so about role play');
- connect the NQT to other support, such as the LEA, NATE or UKRA, all of which may have local activities;
- connect the NQT to teachers in other local schools.

These areas become even more important when the LEA itself is reducing its provision. Local teacher associations, such as NATE, or the local HEI may be some of the few sources of external ideas and support that are available for an NQT (and for a mentor, come to that). Given how exhausting the first years of teaching can be, the departmental mentor may have to play a very proactive role in helping the NQT to look up above the proverbial parapet and to make use of these external stimuli. The mentor may even have to go further and help the NQT to realize that English teachers in other schools have vast amounts to offer. I remember how much I learned in my second year of teaching by managing to visit three local schools to look at how they organized their departmental resources: I benefited, my department benefited and, most importantly, the children benefited the most.

Inspection is now the most demanding aspect of external 'inputs'. It is possible that the inspection team is either relatively 'local' or contains at least one member of the LEA team, but it is just as likely that all the team members are complete strangers to the school and its staff. Either way, the inspection process is highly demanding and unnerving for all the staff. *English and the Ofsted Experience* (Bibby and Wade, 1995) gives a very useful account of the whole process that I shall draw on below. By now the great majority of readers will be familiar with the process, either at first hand or through the experiences of local colleagues.

Whatever its many faults, the current inspection process brings a whole school, and a department in particular, into a close and intense relationship. For NQTs, the inspection is especially nerve wracking because they are inexperienced, but this is partly balanced by the fact that they have usually been frequently observed in the recent past; being observed and criticized is something they are relatively familiar with. This recent experience is of use to the rest of the department, and an NQT can usefully brief the department about the process. However, where the departmental mentor may play an especially valuable role is in helping the NQT to prepare; for example, talking over lesson plans and aspects of department policies that the NQT feels unclear about, or just helping that 'junior' individual to feel confident. One teacher quoted in the *English and the Ofsted Experience* explained how he felt on the morning of the inspection, two years into his career: 'I do remember feeling quite numb as I walked in. We sat in the staff room because we had a briefing beforehand. And as the team was introduced I could feel my stomach churning. I had a lesson beforehand which I don't know how I taught' (Bibby and Wade, 1995: 18). Equally, the NQT may need rather more support after the inspection. The same teacher commented, 'I found it deeply frustrating that I couldn't discuss lessons with the inspector. I can't see why professionals can't sit down and talk about lessons and open the gateway to professional development. To have someone of Colin Forster's [the English inspector's] experience come in and not be able to comment to me on what he saw is just loopy' (Bibby and Wade, 1995: 22). The NQT, like the rest of the team, will receive the overall feedback and also any specific feedback from the inspector's oral report to the head of department, but may need more support and reassurance than more senior staff. Ofsted also has to establish where NQTs received their training and whether they feel that the NQTs have been adequately prepared to teach. In other words, it is to build up a database of HEI 'output', looking specifically for weaknesses – this seems a little ironic when PGCE students spend most of their time in one or two schools, rather than at a particular HEI. However, this is a factor that will no doubt have an eventual impact on the system.

A departmental mentor can only do so much to help an NQT or a student teacher in the turmoil of an inspection, but there are some rather different issues to consider for members of partnership schools. First of all, student teachers can be observed by inspectors and questioned about their perceptions of their progress and of the support that they receive from their school and their HEI. In simple terms then, Ofsted is not really interested in the students themselves but is looking to make judgements about the quality of school-based teacher education. The school, and therefore its mentors, is coming under some scrutiny of the ways in which it provides for student teachers. However, the real issue appears to be the HEI institutions, how they are 'performing' and teachers' perceptions of them. An underlying, though not publicly declared, issue in all this is for Ofsted to evaluate the readiness of schools to take on teacher education entirely. This, after all, is the logical conclusion of the view of teacher apprenticeships, outlined in Chapter 1.

Readers must make up their own minds about the value of the HE contribution to teacher education and about whether current partnership arrangements offer the best approach now and in the medium term. All I am alerting them to is the need to recognize that inspections have many purposes, some explicit and clear, others rather more shadowy. It may well be that the special kinds of meeting that schools and departments now hold to prepare for inspection should include their partnership role on the agenda, and that those individuals, including the students themselves, who are directly involved in school-based teacher education might need distinct meetings to focus on particular issues. If teacher education is part of the fabric of the school, this attention to it in relation to an inspection makes perfect sense. If I am making a special case, then unashamedly I say that a special case needs to be made, especially in the short term. Schools are likely to be the final arbiters of the long-term future of teacher education and I am quite certain that the readers of this book would not want their views misrepresented. A collation of hundreds of casual comments, elicited apparently in passing references to school-based teacher education, would not, in my opinion, provide a sound basis for professional judgement; nor should it pretend that professional judgements had been consulted. If readers feel that I am unconsciously revealing my fears of dark conspiracies then they can relax, because I am perfectly conscious that I do fear such conspiracies and that I am right to do so. There is simply too much evidence to be able to ignore it.

In-service training

With student teachers, the main role for the mentor is in making sure that they take an active role in any in-service days that coincide with their time in school. As these days vary so much in their style and their content, the above suggestion is about the only useful generalization. It has at least become the normal expectation that student teachers should not only attend but that, on occasion, they may even be slightly better informed than some staff and so may actually contribute rather than simply be present. If a particular day has a departmental focus, then student teachers stand to gain a great deal of insight into current practice. Even on departmental days student teachers may have something substantial to offer. In areas such as media education and information technology students can sometimes be excellent providers of in-service. It is certainly worth the mentor's time to establish what might be achieved on such an occasion through the full involvement of the students. With such an approach everyone stands to gain, and the mentor is providing opportunities for professional development for all staff. These points apply equally to NQTs, although it may be even more important to give them specific, contributory roles on in-service days, so that they feel valued and can grow in professional confidence.

The departmental mentor has a fuller role to play with NQTs in helping them to identify suitable in-service provision outside the school. As we have considered above, this process can be a very productive aspect of the mentor–mentee dialogue and part of our collective long-term strategy for the development of the whole profession. In this spirit we can move on to the final chapter, which seeks to put student teachers, NQTs and experienced teachers into a continuum, examining the principles that might help us to develop a truly reflective profession.

6 Developing ourselves: English teachers and continuous professional development

A professional development continuum

One of the greatest gains of HEI and school partnerships, at least where the partnership is providing high-quality school-based teacher education, is the simple, but crucial, opportunity to view teaching generally and, for us, English teaching in particular as a professional *continuum*. I am not claiming that this is a new idea but, ironically, it is, in its way, a surprisingly radical one. The simplest way to illustrate this would be to point up, as I am sure most readers know, that 'career development' for teachers is incredibly haphazard and can be almost entirely up to the proactive individual. This is a very broad generalization and I am aware of many English departments and many schools where professional development is taken very seriously indeed. However, over the profession as a whole, there is much that is haphazard and unplanned. For example, what career path exists for the teacher who simply wants to get better at teaching? I shall return to this point in much more depth later in the chapter.

We examined appraisal in Chapter 5 and recognized that it has considerable potential in a number of ways to help give teacher's careers more sense of planned continuity and development, but that, as a mechanism in schools, it has a very long way to go to become an established means to that end. One of the particular difficulties for schools is that if they do appraise someone as very successful in the classroom they may find themselves with nothing to offer but praise. Encouragement and praise are always valuable, but they do not provide the *challenge* that successful teachers are usually looking for.

At the time of writing, all the political parties are talking about teaching as a career, particularly as pupil numbers are rising sharply and as teachers are becoming harder to recruit and many are retiring earlier. The politicians are thus looking, typically and understandably, for inexpensive ways to improve the quality of teaching as a career. Some of this talk may turn into practical realities and even opportunities, but there is a looming crisis in the profession that needs facing. Some measures will have to be taken.

One very important factor in this rather gloomy picture is the trend of the late 1980s and into the 1990s of reducing both teacher autonomy and, to some extent, teacher status. Most so-called consultations of the profession have been derisory and superficial;[1] the Dearing Reports of 1995 and 1996 are worthwhile exceptions. For example, teachers everywhere initially welcomed the National Curriculum framework but many teachers, English teachers in particular, were most unhappy with its *prescriptive content*. Since that time (1988/9), most changes to the curriculum affecting English, especially those to do with assessment, have been resisted and rejected by English teachers. Nevertheless, these changes have come into being. Such a heavy-handed and dogmatic approach to change has been demoralizing and demotivating. In a curious way there could be no greater tribute to English teachers' genuine and selfless professionalism than that they have kept going in the face of such relentlessly difficult and chaotic circumstances. However, there have been real losses and many English teachers continue to be highly dissatisfied with what has happened. For some there has been the real question of whether they want to continue an English teaching career at all.

I began this chapter with the positive point that the best types of partnership scheme may help us with long-term professional development, and the purpose of this chapter is to look closely at this idea. Despite all the negative points above about what has been done unto teachers, it is a positive chapter and looks forward with some real optimism, but it is neither naive nor innocent in its approach. The nature of change in education, especially in secondary schooling in particular, has been once more to highlight that many of the best changes for teachers have come *from teachers*; the introduction of coursework and oral work in English seem perfect examples of this point. This chapter then examines how the individual teacher can *continue to develop*. The models of development I shall discuss are not isolationist, however. On the contrary, they are very much social and collegiate ones. Teachers need to work closely with each other and with other colleagues who can stimulate and sustain professional development. My final point, at this stage, is that I aim to conclude the book by placing the concept of mentorship within this idea of the continuum of development. In order to achieve this we will need to review aspects of the idea, and the ideal, of the reflective practitioner and to consider what contribution mentorship can make to that ideal.

The reflective practitioner revisited: entering the hall of mirrors

I discussed the concept of the reflective practitioner in Chapter 2, but pointed out that for the purposes of that chapter it was best to focus very specifically, and I hope appropriately, on its implications for student teachers and for mentorship. Here I wish to look closely at certain key ideas about reflective practice in more depth, although the implications for mentorship are just as considerable and will be discussed fully further on.

Student teachers, as we examined in Chapter 2, can be reflective and can develop the capacity to reflect as they become more understanding about teaching and learning through being 'in the action'. We have reviewed a whole range of ways of helping them, consciously most of the time, to become increasingly reflective. For the experienced teacher, the interaction with the student herself, or equally with a novice teacher, can be an excellent stimulus to reflection; her uncertainties and questions helping the 'old hand' (however chronologically young) to look afresh at the familiar features of the classroom, discovering, perhaps, new possibilities. However, such 'freshness' comes from hard work and the demanding capacity to rethink, being reflective sounds straight forward but certainly is not in practice. Schön comments (quoted in Grimmet and Erikson, 1988: 23) on how we all need help to be reflective, and that we can be coached in reflection, especially by someone who is close to the teacher's or student teacher's action. 'The coach joins a teacher in her reflection on her own reflection-in-action, seeks to enter into a kind of collaborative on-the spot research, and creates a Hall of Mirrors in which coaching illustrates what it is about.' One important element in this chapter is to look at what we know about being a reflective practitioner in order to be, in the true sense, a model for others.

However, the concept of the reflective practitioner is not actually uncontroversial in itself. Most busy teachers inevitably know of the work of Donald Schön through secondary sources, and the term 'reflective practitioner' is in some danger of becoming a cliché, a phrase worn out through too casual use. However, there are some who contest Schön's ideas, and also far more who are unhappy with the current nature of his definition and who are trying to use his basic concept to find a definition that they think will be more accurate and more useful to the profession generally.[2] This questioning of his pioneering work is exactly what some researchers should be doing, and may well lead to a reconceptualization of the definition. Teachers reading this section are alerted, I hope, to their active role here. We are all searching for ways of understanding how really good teaching 'works' and, as a profession, need to keep an open mind at all times. The following ideas about long-term reflective practice are just that, ideas. They are based on Dewey's original thinking,[3] and then on Schön's conception, on other sources and research and on my own experience in classrooms full of children or student teachers, sometimes both. They are also based on working closely over the years with colleagues who, to me, have shown in action and in their conversation that they are truly reflective practitioners, individuals who have certainly entered the hall of mirrors. We are all potentially involved in working towards a better understanding of what we mean by 'reflective practice'. There is plenty more to do on the topic.

The other point here, familiar but important, is that, despite all this rhetoric about reflective practitioners, there is little reward for being one, except the intrinsic value to the individual. Being an 'ordinary' classroom teacher has almost negative, connotations whereas having a title – head of department, coordinator of Key Stage 3, in charge of drama – confers both status and, usually, some financial recognition. Distractions like half-baked notions of 'performance-related pay' offer no useful way forward as they are currently envisaged. This lack of recognition for the accomplished teacher is a serious concern, and certainly has a limiting effect on professional growth. I shall focus in the next section on some initiatives that seek to redress this imbalance.

Given these points, first that 'reflective practice' is not a neat formula that everyone can adopt and second that being a 'career teacher' almost militates against becoming one, it does seem vital to offer a considered framework for becoming a reflective practitioner.

John Dewey (1933) characterized reflection as a *specialized form of thinking*. He argued that its starting point is doubt and perplexity felt in a *directly experienced situation*. This perplexity leads on to *purposeful inquiry* and *problem resolution*. During reflection we draw on our evidence from the past and test its reliability. We need to determine a new course of action, bearing in mind this existing evidence. He is always clear that we must accept the paradoxical condition of reflection, that we cannot know without acting and that we cannot act without knowing. Therefore we try to *get hold* of the problem or doubt that we now experience. This *uncertainty draws out reflection* and we look for a solution. We may well find our solution but we are, by being reflective, accepting that experience and action are problematics; our solutions will be useful but tentative. Dewey is careful to use the term *observations*. These are our data, which are not accidental, but are acquired through observing and leads us to take time to hypothesize possibilities. At this stage we have to endure some suspense. We do not rush into action, as we systematically consider our bank of knowledge and, after critical scrutiny of what we know and what we might do, we can imagine possibilities that have the nature of predictions but without a narrow sense of certainty. Once we try out our chosen course of action there is a good chance that we will transform the uncertainty into some kind of clarity and coherence. For a time, the problem is resolved.

Crucially for Dewey, reflection is very different from acquiring information. He conceptualizes acquiring information as very much the simple process of memory. What reflection does, at least potentially, is transform information into knowledge, and knowledge leads to wisdom, leading ultimately to the better living of life. Wisdom is not, however, a final and rigid state of certainty. One of its most powerful elements is that it makes us clear sighted. Such clarity means, paradoxically, that we can see the messiness and perplexity of life as just that. Dewey's work has been, and continues to be, immensely influential. What Schön's work has done is to take Dewey's large-scale, philosophical conception and to try to focus it on actual practitioners, working in their field.

He has explored a number of professions, seeking to find universals in their work. Here I shall focus on his ideas as he has applied them to teachers.

One of Schön's key ideas is that what constitutes the subject, say English teaching, can only really be found in the knowledge-in-action of practitioners; their professional actions and their reflection upon them, both while teaching (reflection-in-action) and while outside the classroom (reflection-on-action), are where the field is developing. Schön generally plays down what he terms *technical rationality*, which I take to mean purely abstract, theoretical thinking. In other words, you will not learn to be a good English teacher by reading about it but by doing it and reflecting on what you are doing and have done. Schön considers that much genuine reflective practice is comparable to artistic, intuitive processes; it is a *creative process*. Teachers are thus experimenting as artists do, searching for better technique and better expression. This is often a messy and indeterminate process, not always conscious. To pursue the artistic metaphor further, teachers need to *frame* what is going on in order to capture it. They need to *set* the problem which their uncertainty about a professional practice has produced in order to find ways of resolving it. 'When we set the problem, we select what we will treat as the "things" of the situation, we set the boundaries of our attention to it, and we impose upon it a coherence which allows us to say what is wrong and in what directions the situation needs to be changed. Problem setting is a process in which, interactively, we *name* the things to which we will attend and *frame* the context in which we will attend to them' (Schön, 1983: 40).

This is not a static situation. Schön terms it 'a conversation'. Drawing directly on Dewey, he formulates how we bring all our experience and repertoire of examples, images, understandings and actions to bear on this problematic situation. 'In this reflective conversation, the practitioner's effort to solve the reframed problem yields new discoveries which call for new reflection-in-action. The process spirals through stages of appreciation, action and reappreciation. The unique and uncertain situation comes to be understood through the attempt to change it, and changed through the attempt to understand it' (Schön, 1983: 132).

The final aspect of Schön's work that we need to review here is his insistence on *experimentation*. He sees this as one hallmark of the genuine reflective practitioner. In this way, a teacher is always questioning what the appropriate action to take is in a problematic situation. This idea does not refute much of our earlier discussion of how skilful teachers become unconsciously competent. We only have so much attention to give consciously to our practice, so the reflective teacher is setting the boundaries of a particular problem in order to give it full, conscious attention. This selected area of attention is where the 'experimenting' can take place.

I support much of Schön's thinking but wish to add one corrective and one simple point of my own at this stage. One of Schön's great strengths, as with Dewey, is that he is an enthusiast for change and improvement, aiming, as

Dewey so powerfully expresses it, to help us all towards 'the better living of life'. For Schön there is a kind of imagined enemy, the abstract theoretician, divorced from the messiness of action and unappreciative of truly professional practice. Therefore, much of Schön's work is highly, and enjoyably, rhetorical and argumentative. It constantly quarrels with this abstract enemy. I recognize that enemy, knowing that he (they usually are male) will always exist. However, I am just as concerned about the other enemy, the one whose rhetoric comes from the opposite end of the spectrum and who would argue that teachers simply deliver the National Curriculum and that, if they have a degree in their subject, they need think no more and can just 'get on with it'. These opposites are a kind of dialectic and I think we have learned enough to have some form of synthesis.

I think we have moved on and I think school-based teacher education is a perfect example of what might be an excellent kind of synthesis. My 'corrective' point is that Schön, in attempting to win his particular argument, has somewhat overstated the case. Partly through his work, and that of like-minded others, we have come to a far clearer conception of how practitioners shape and reshape the domains they work in. We have come to recognize that reflective practitioners are developing the subject and are experimenting with possibilities. Those practitioners who take, as it were, one step away from the field, such as subject advisers, do not cease to exist; their contribution, in certain cases, may be far greater to reflecting on and developing the subject because they are a stimulus to others and are also able to gain from the numerous individual reflections of many teachers. I remain far more concerned about the second enemy, the one who thinks that teaching does not require much thought and is, indeed, rather worried when teachers display thinking tendencies, such as questioning the wisdom of aspects of the National Curriculum.

The other point through which I show some disagreement with Schön is simple. I would argue that reflective practitioners, as well as attempting to solve the problems they encounter through their own work, inevitably look for other stimuli to reflection, outside that daily context. Some of those stimuli will come from reading and from considering, quite consciously, radical challenges to practice that can only be, initially, *theoretical*; that is to say, not fully tried out. A crucial point for me, which will be explored in the next section, but that has had some attention already throughout this book, is the recognition by the true reflective practitioner of the theory (or theories) both implicit and explicit in their practice. I think it most unlikely that a practitioner can be fully reflective, at this profound level, until she has the right combination of professional experience and stimulus to reflection.

Schön's hall of mirrors is an interesting metaphor because such a place is actually designed to be confusing and disorientating, intended more to amuse us than to make us think. However, it is a metaphor that reminds me about individual autonomy. It is, after all, an unusual experience to see ourselves, as others see us all the time, from several angles and in peculiarly distorted ways. We may simply be amused, which can be enough in itself; we may 'learn' something from it, but only if we consciously, and rather more seriously, attend to what we see, revealed in the mirrors. A good mentor has the courage to enter that difficult place and to know that everyone who does may see something new as a result. The mentor of course has the added responsibility of being a guide for those who may find the experience very confusing.

The anxiety of expertise

A thread throughout this text is teachers' tendency towards humility. In a positive light this is a kind of thoughtful modesty and much to be respected and admired in itself. However, as I have stressed before, I think that it has been taken very great advantage of over the past few years and, in the rather harsh and unfriendly spotlight cast by politicians and the media, it is perhaps in danger of becoming, however unjustly, a form of so-called 'contributory negligence'. Teaching generally is becoming a less attractive option for bright and enthusiastic people, whether young or mature. There are many reasons for this, and some of them are to do with the relative decline in teachers' salaries as the economy has gradually recovered. I have always found the 'But think of all the holidays' comment about teaching somewhat ironic if you cannot afford to take one. My main concern here is not with all the socio-economic factors affecting people's choice of profession but rather with self-image. Why do teachers themselves tend to downplay their achievements and especially their classroom expertise?

Most good teachers, in my opinion, are highly expert and full of profes-sional wisdom, and I wish I could do more to demonstrate this simple point. But how do I 'know'? What do such teachers do, in their daily work, to demonstrate this expertise? I do not have a complete answer and I think, as with Schön's conception of the reflective practitioner, that we have not arrived yet but that we are finding ways to understand what real expertise in teaching consists of. It will always be much easier to spot poor teaching, to say why it is poor and, possibly, to find ways to improve it. Recognizing excellent teach-ing, understanding why it is excellent and still looking to improve it is a far greater challenge. The next section examines this ideal. It is intended to help readers whose motive in being a mentor is to be a good mentor and a better teacher, and, even more difficult, to face the anxiety and the responsibility, as well as the great excitement and challenge, of being a role model within the profession.

Identifying 'highly accomplished teachers'

There has been work on the idea of the expert teacher in several English-speaking countries over the past few years, notably the USA and Australia.[4] I am certain that there is far more research and development work to be done before we can arrive at any kind of consensual definition of the expert teacher, even though there has already been enough development in this field to produce another book. Currently there is no formal recognition in the UK of excellence in teaching, and the profession generally has, quite rightly, wished to avoid simplistic, performance-related models, especially linked to crude outcomes like examination results. As discussed earlier in reference to *The Making of English Teachers* (Protherough and Atkinson, 1991), many practitioners considered successful by their peers will study for advanced qualifications and these will tend to be higher degrees. What we have, so far, in terms of qualifications, is a lack of any attempt to recognize and celebrate classroom expertise by using *the teacher's classroom* as the chief focus. Teachers studying for higher degrees are constantly encouraged to undertake systematic research in their classrooms, and I am one of those people directly involved in encouraging and enjoying such excellent and professionally productive work. The dissertation work, in particular of some masters students, contains classroom-based research of the highest quality. However, I have felt for a long time that in looking for a continuum of professional development, there is a need to provide something that focuses more directly on a teacher's everyday work; work that may be everyday but is, in fact, far from ordinary.

In this, relatively brief, section I am simply going to summarize the work of an initiative based at the University of Reading in the UK. This initiative is seeking to create an Advanced Certificate in the Teaching of English, in other words to recognize and celebrate the achievement of outstanding teachers of English.[5] I offer it here as a contribution to our developing understanding of teaching expertise, in the spirit of Schön's conversation, as something that I hope will provoke some reflection and response in readers. I do not offer it as exclusive or definitive but I do think it offers some real potential for adding to the continuum of professional development.

To introduce this concept I want first to provide some contextualization. There can be no such thing as *the* definitive expert teacher any more than there is, say, *the* definitive expert footballer. There are expert footballers aplenty but readers will be aware that football pundits debate endlessly about who is the best. Equally, footballers are sub-divided into forwards, midfielders and defenders, and then further sub-divisions and categories exist. They will all have some generic skills in common but they will also be different in specific skills. Expert teachers will be similar, and therefore characterization of expert teaching needs to bear in mind commonality and diversity, and even the crucial but inevitably problematic issue of originality. When people become genuinely expert they have reached a stage in which they might well wish to challenge the rather conventional wisdom of others; this fits well with Schön's ideas that reflective practitioners are genuinely creating new knowledge and any system intending to recognize expert teachers needs to be open enough to acknowledge unusual and very individual insights.

A second point is that if one is setting out to evaluate expert teaching one has to decide how to 'get hold of it', especially as much of it happens 'in action', during lessons. Any assessment or recognition system needs to be sensitive to the contexts of teaching and to the deep personal knowledge that expert teachers have of their students and their context. Such a system will also need to be rigorous. If teachers are to carry the status of being 'expert' then their peers will want the reassurance that the experts have been properly, and fairly, assessed. Readers will already recognize the complexities and difficulties in such a process.

The outline below was put together by a group of English teachers, a teacher educator and an LEA inspector for English (see note 5).

Personal characteristics

The highly accomplished teacher is:

- self-reflective and self-critical;
- prepared to experiment;
- able to provide appropriate guidance and response;
- tolerant and promotes tolerance amongst pupils;
- an excellent communicator, clear, articulate and responsive to others.

The highly accomplished teacher is able to:

- teach all abilities;
- make learning accessible;
- motivate, challenge and stimulate pupils;
- encourage all pupils to achieve high standards;
- recognize individual needs and respond appropriately;
- select materials appropriately;
- support critically;
- handle sensitive issues;
- promote pupils' spiritual, moral and social development;
- manage pupils' behaviour;
- draw on a wide range of subject resources.

Professional identity

The highly accomplished teacher has:

- a strong background in the field of English and/or English teaching;
- an active involvement in English teaching within the whole school and beyond the school;
- a demonstrated interest in professional development;
- an ability to envisage change and development within the subject and to be an agent in that process;

- the respect of colleagues;
- the potential to be a role model for, or mentor of, other teachers.

Subject knowledge

The highly accomplished teacher:

- has a thorough understanding of English as a subject within the secondary school;
- has a good understanding of the complex and controversial nature of English;
- is enthusiastic for, and shows commitment to, the subject;
- keeps abreast of and responds to changes to the subject;
- is able to understand a range of texts;
- is able to develop pupil's reading and response skills (for example the development of reading skills, or in writing, developing sense of audience and context, and in speaking and listening too);
- is able to develop speaking and listening skills;
- can teach about different genres, styles, structures, forms of rhetoric etc., e.g. how to write persuasively;
- can identify/recognize different models of effective writing, speaking etc.;
- knows how language is developed through all four modes;
- is aware of relevant theory (e.g. subject, psychology, learning) and incorporates such understandings in practice;
- has a thorough knowledge of the National Curriculum for English.

Planning and review

The highly accomplished teacher:

- ensures that aims and objectives are both challenging and realistic and are communicated clearly to pupils;
- plans effectively in the short and long term;
- can follow plans closely while retaining a sensitivity to contextual issues and individual children;
- produces coherent and comprehensive plans and schemes.

Assessment and recording

The highly accomplished teacher:

- is able to recognize each individual's achievement;
- understands stages of development and ensures progression;
- maintains accurate records of pupils' progress;
- has a broad understanding of a range of possible assessment techniques.

Documentation

The highly accomplished teacher:

- prepares classroom materials of high quality;
- develops effective teaching resources for others' use;
- contributes to the development of departmental guidelines and policy statements.

Relationships with pupils and colleagues

In relation to pupils the highly accomplished teacher:

- is an excellent facilitator;
- promotes thinking;
- promotes increasing independence and autonomy;
- stimulates pupils' enjoyment and interest;
- differentiates through knowledge of individual children.

In relation to colleagues, the highly accomplished teacher:

- works collaboratively with others;
- seeks contacts outside the immediate environment;
- shares good practice;
- enjoys peer respect.

Contextual understanding

The highly accomplished teacher:

- understands the place of English within the local and National Curriculum;
- is familiar with school aims and policies;
- understands the school in relation to its catchment area, to local circumstances and to the linguistic and social backgrounds of pupils;
- communicates effectively with parents;
- understands the school's relationships with local groups and agencies.

Such a list is daunting but, much more importantly, it helps us to see that highly accomplished teaching is extraordinarily sophisticated and subtle. It also brings home, I hope, the earlier point about difference. Expert teachers really are like this description, but none of us are likely to be at an equal level in every aspect. This does not mean that such expertise cannot be recognized and acknowledged. We have put forward, at this stage, some ways of 'getting hold' of expert teaching.

Some types of evidence and means of collection

- classroom observation;
- previous or other observations, e.g. appraisals;

- video recording of teaching;
- teacher's own writing, e.g. plans and schemes, evaluations, reflective commentaries on videos of the classroom, analysis of critical incidents, commentaries on individual pupils and their work, a reflective diary;
- teacher's responding to case studies, articles about key issues within English teaching;
- interviews with the teacher;
- portfolio of evidence containing some or all of the above.

Evidence for particular categories

Documentation:

- quality of plans and pupils' work;
- evidence of progress.

Subject knowledge:

- record of work done, plans, intentions, resources;
- written schemes of work;
- INSET record;
- coursework/research, making reference to other research;
- in seminar presentations and discussions.

Methodological:

- observation;
- reflective notes;
- video;
- peer assessment, colleagues in school and on a course;
- pupil response, notes, interview, demeanour, product, feedback;
- HoD/head/SMT report;
- elected headteacher assessor from consortium of schools.

Management skills:

- observation/video;
- scrutiny of planning, explicit to classroom management within planning;
- reflective log/diary/commentary/evaluation;
- appraisal.

Relationships:

- observation with a class, discussion with colleagues (component of wider report);
- teacher's own commentary and comments from others.

This description is only a beginning and much work remains to be done to refine and improve it. However, we feel it goes some way towards capturing the truly remarkable skills of the highly accomplished teacher of English. I hope that it also serves to remind mentors of just how much student teachers have to learn and, also, how they can never learn all of this in 24 weeks in school. A mentor cannot hope to communicate all these skills to a student teacher, even though they may all be present in her work. However, the reflective mentor, the true role model, can make much more conscious use of these remarkable skills by being the true reflective practitioner and by systematically reviewing her practice. As we have identified, we all need help in reflection, and a highly accomplished teacher still needs that help. Along with this written framework, such a teacher will still need the equivalent of mentoring, and at this 'level', the equivalence might be offered by a peer who adopts the mentoring role for that purpose. I shall return to this point.

The above material should help readers to review their own practice and to evaluate it in a way *meaningful to them*. If being a role model for student teachers, beginning teachers and colleagues involved demonstrating all these qualities then none of us would take on the 'job'. My chief point here is that for good teachers the framework helps to identify strengths and to point up areas where the individual wants to improve. As has been stressed a number of times in this text, if we are expert then we are likely to need help to bring some of that expertise to the conscious level, and especially if we want to identify an area to work on systematically. Our 'attention', being necessarily selective, means that we must focus on what we can undertake and evaluate in *a conscious way*. A useful analogy here, especially for mentors, is that most drivers, however expert, recognize that they may have developed one or two 'bad' habits. These habits become quite obvious when someone points them out or, importantly, when the driver in question is trying to teach someone else how to drive and is confronted with her own sloppiness or laziness in some area of their driving. A corrective to this, rather negative, point is that those who are truly reflective practitioners (and drivers) are keen to examine their practice and will welcome means of achieving improvement, especially if they respect the *means to reflection*. The section above attempts to provide such a means and might form the basis for discussion at department meetings and with peers, i.e. highly accomplished colleagues. It will also provide a basis for the final sections of the book, as I conclude with an argument for a reflective cycle, informing the continuum of professional development.

To return briefly to the driving metaphor, in my own experience, I do not usually respond comfortably to the occasional negative comment about my driving by other experienced drivers. I accept that this is partly to do with my character, but it is also to do with the situation. Such comments may be well intentioned and even be accompanied by an 'endearment': 'Aren't you a bit close to that lorry, darling?' but they are not usually productive of the desired effect. Like almost everyone else I am more receptive in other circumstances and I really do want to drive as well as possible. So, if highly accomplished peers are to help each other then they do need a means and a framework.

Taking on the *mentoring role* – that is, to adopt its stance and its purpose – may be a way of making real, positive use of the focus it brings to the participants. This may be especially true if the situation can be defined by some agreed characteristics. I discuss these characteristics below. Further, the peer who adopts the *mentee stance* can, perhaps simply by commenting on the characteristics in relation to herself, try to make explicit where she feels she is and where she might go to improve.

Ultimately, I am suggesting that teachers who become experienced as mentors should be able to draw on the skills of mentoring even when working in a peer situation. Given that even the most accomplished teacher will want to improve, we need to find ways and means of providing that help. In a reflective profession we can become skilful at helping each other, even when we are already very good. We can be much better and more sophisticated than offering the occasional 'back seat driver' comment.

Becoming a 'highly accomplished teacher'

The focus of this book is chiefly on one key aspect of highly accomplished teaching, and this aspect, the mentorship role, is the subject of this section.

For student and beginning teachers there are many potential role models, but there is none so powerful as the successful classroom teacher. Teacher educators have their considerable part to play in student teachers' development but a classroom teacher is 'the real thing'; teacher educators are well aware that once they have the university/college 'status', they have instantly lost much of what might be called their 'classroom cred'. I am not suggesting that either teacher educators or mentors merely accept such narrow definitions of each other's role, and we can all be aware of the potentially damaging effects that such simplistic views can cause. In fact, my experience of the great majority of the mentors that I have worked with is that they actively discourage such views, especially in their student teachers. What I am emphasizing here is that both mentors and teacher educators are operating in a climate where such narrow views often prevail, so we can be apprised of them and get on with the basic job of helping the student teachers themselves. Changing the 'climate' requires a much longer-term strategy.

The highly accomplished classroom teacher of English is therefore, potentially at least, the key *role model* for the aspiring student or beginning teacher. However modest teachers may be about their expertise, there is no doubt that they need to be *conscious role models* if they want to make a difference to the professional novices who seek, to some extent, to emulate them. Emulation is a very important word here, being very different from mere imitation. Being a role model goes beyond being a mentor. It requires more of the individual and stretches that individual in every way. I recognize that this is not a position that some teachers, however good, may want to accept.

Jerome Bruner (1966) has pointed out that experts are able to demonstrate things with great skill, but that they often disguise difficulty, unintentionally, by making things look easy. So, he argues, a *good demonstration* is not one that makes the activity look easy but one that reveals its difficulty in a meaningful way. Much of this book has examined this issue in relation to the classroom, but this section now argues for a wider remit. Being a real role model involves demonstrating much that lies outside the direct provenance of the classroom and illuminates the much wider domain of the professional who is reflective, and also visibly *active*.

The previous section may be considered, without making a definitive claim for it, as something of a blueprint for a role model in English teaching, and although its comprehensiveness is daunting, it is a true picture of what such teachers are like. I would suggest that being a role model is made easier, rather than more difficult, by inclusion of the mentorship dimension within it. Taking Bruner's point about demonstration, a good role model will help a less accomplished colleague to recognize difficulties but not to feel even more daunted by them. As with an obvious physical skill like juggling, novices look and feel hopeless and then may suddenly make a breakthrough that allows them to develop much more quickly and to begin to 'look good'. A role model is not therefore saying 'Look how good I am' but, instead 'Look, this is really difficult, let us look together at how to do it. Some of the time I will inevitably make it look easy but I am still learning myself.' If anything, the role model's stress actually needs to be on *her own learning*. If student teachers, beginning teachers and less accomplished colleagues are really going to be a part of a continuum of professional development, then it is essential that those further along that continuum demonstrate their wish to be still moving. This is just as true of teacher educators, who have an equal responsibility to show their open-mindedness and eagerness to learn. Demonstrating such a dedication to learning and self-development may take a number of forms, although the most obvious will usually be studying for advanced qualifications.

The UK is rather unusual as a Western nation, in that relatively few of its teachers have higher degrees. In the USA, in contrast, it is most unusual for an experienced teacher to be without at least a masters degree. In fact, in many states it is compulsory to obtain one, and in others there is no chance of promotion without such a qualification. It is quite true that the system of higher education there is substantially different and that there are direct rewards for teachers, mostly financial ones, for obtaining higher degrees, so a strict comparison cannot be made.

However, for whatever reasons, most UK English teachers do not choose this route to personal development. In *The Making of English Teachers* (Protherough and Atkinson, 1991), the authors carried out a survey of teachers nominated by their peers as 'particularly effective English practitioners'. Of that group, over 52 per cent already had a higher degree or advanced diploma and 'a good number were at present engaged in taking advanced courses leading towards an award' (*ibid.*: 23). Neither the authors nor I would suggest that there is a strict correlation between being a 'particularly effective English practitioner' and having a higher degree or its equivalent. However, it is striking that so many people nominated by their peers as good *practitioners* should also have advanced qualifications.

From my own perspective, after many years of running a higher degree for English teachers, I can only add how much I have enjoyed working with such dedicated and energetic people. I am too closely involved and associated with that particular course to feel that I should use it as a main part of my argument here. What I can say is that my experience fits with that documented by Protherough and Atkinson. The real role models, the true reflective practitioners, are concerned to stretch themselves to the full, and a higher degree is one excellent means of achieving this end. It may be considered as one fairly typical characteristic of expert teachers and of those teachers who are highly respected by their peers; those, in other words, who are role models.

There is a long-term professional issue here too, although not a simple one. Teaching has steadily been moving towards all graduate status, something that is reflected in the structure of the profession, including its financial system. There is, however, certainly no neat correlation between having a degree and being a good teacher, and, as I have already examined at length, there are all too many simplistic views about subject knowledge as opposed to subject pedagogical knowledge, some held by student teachers, which undervalue the true professionalism of teachers themselves. However, there is a real distinction to be made between simplistic views about teaching and the importance of having *a highly qualified profession*. Once teachers have achieved their base line newly qualified status, the very great majority are going to have both a subject degree (or its equivalent) and an appropriate teaching qualification. At this stage, at least in the majority of cases, the simplistic models of teaching will have disappeared.

It seems entirely sensible, for a country that wants to have a highly educated population, to have a highly educated teaching profession. I do not need to tell readers of this book that becoming highly qualified is problematic. There are very few resources targeted at this area. There are no longer any full-time secondments, which means that teachers not only have to study part-time while working full-time, but, generally, they have to pay for some qualifications themselves. This is not true for most comparable professions, but I see little value here in spending more time on this issue, except to sum up that it would be highly beneficial for the profession if matters were different and so were more favourable to teachers' long-term professional development.

The simple point is that, for whatever reasons, teaching is a well qualified profession but not, currently, a highly qualified one. This point is, as I outlined above, a long-term concern for the whole profession. For mentors seeking to be role models, undertaking an extended qualification, like a higher degree, is one very visible way of demonstrating commitment and professionalism.

It is not the only way, and for most teachers who work with such role models, the evidence of expertise will emerge in professional conversations with colleagues. I have pointed out that student teachers 'enjoy' these conversations all the time, have their classrooms visited regularly and are used to observers and a variety of team teaching strategies. For the vast majority of English teachers their working life is dominated by the paradox of being constantly surrounded by crowds, yet being alone; literally the only reasonable adult in a sometimes unruly crowd. In creating a continuum of professional development we need to recognize the limiting effects of such isolation and plan to compensate for such effects. In this effort the individual teacher's department becomes the crucial context for professional development.

Reflective departments

It is perfectly possible for good teachers to work in a relatively ineffective department, although such inequities are unlikely to coexist for long because such teachers inevitably tend to 'make things happen', outside the classroom as well as in it. Perhaps, twenty years ago, some English departments might have had several very good teachers but no real department to speak of; individuals pursued their own paths and there was, apparently, little need for a team of teachers. It would be tedious for readers to rehearse all the demands on English as a subject that have made efficient departments a necessity in order to cope, principally, with bureaucratic systems. Administrative efficiency is a great thing and I have nothing but respect for it, but no good teacher would confuse it with good English teaching or a good department. Any good department, and school, will have administrative systems that help with efficiency; they are a means to the end of good learning.

Reflective departments will be efficient places and such environments are especially helpful to student and beginning teachers. Reflective departments are not, however, obsessed with efficiency over, for example, experiment. They will accept, for example, the risks associated with mentoring student teachers who may, or may not, reduce 'efficiency' in the short term. My point is that in looking at the professional development continuum of English teachers, certain features of departments stand out as helpful in creating that continuum. A mentor can, and should, be instrumental in that creation. The following points are based on my own analysis of departments and, as with the section on highly accomplished teaching, they are offered in the spirit of an ongoing professional conversation. I do not claim that they are definitive, but I am happy to defend their validity as a reasonably comprehensive starting point. Any reader can make use of them as the equivalent to a framework for one kind of departmental evaluation.

Reflective departments tend to have:

- Regular department meetings that focus on a range of concerns, not just the necessary business of administration, and including over a period of time:

professional development (e.g. INSET, training days, NATE), planned, proactive change, information about new resources, regular discussions about
aspects of teaching, space for individuals to raise concerns.

- An openness to outsiders, e.g. student teachers, prospective PGCE students, teachers from other schools.
- An interest in hearing the views of those outsiders and learning from their
  observations.
- A clear organization of responsibilities that are shared throughout the department and that are frequently reviewed and revised.
- A structure that identifies the different levels of mentorship operating in
  the team.
- Staff who are actively engaged in their own professional development and
  that of others, e.g. INSET, higher degrees, work for a subject association.

For some departments some of these activities and processes are assisted by
links to one, or more, HEI institutions, but I am not suggesting that such a
link is essential to a reflective department.

The points above speak largely for themselves. In such a department, ongoing professional development is integrated into the department's thinking and
planning. Mentorship is already identified as one key element in the potential
continuum. These factors make the establishment of a reflective cycle a real
possibility.

The reflective cycle: highly accomplished teachers and highly accomplished student teachers

The main thrust of the last part of this book has been towards establishing
a reflective cycle that fosters a continuum of professional development. Not
all departments will have either student teachers or beginning teachers; a few
may actually have only very experienced teachers in the team. However, the
majority of departments experience staff changes quite regularly. Even if changes
are rare and the staff are all experienced, there is never a case for ignoring the
fundamental element in all teachers' work, the teaching itself. What we are
examining is the way that we can keep teaching in the foreground and can
help all teachers, whatever their stage of development, to move on. The idea
of a reflective cycle is, in this sense, one that is appropriate to all English
departments, whatever their staffing situation.

I hope that the last few sections have established the idea that mentoring
and the idea of taking a mentoring stance with peers can be seen as an ongoing
and crucially useful part of this pattern of continuing professional development. It has become a central role in the initial stages of teacher education and
this has helped to raise its profile and its status. This book attempts to go
further and to suggest that this does help to enhance the existing skills of
teachers with student teachers, and so to establish a rather different body of

professional knowledge that can be the basis for future developments with, potentially, all teachers.

The goal is always the same, and that is to move teachers along the continuum. We do all move anyway, to some extent, but we are looking at how we can move *more consciously* and *more successfully*. This is where the reflective cycle comes in. As I have stressed in several earlier sections, teachers frequently emphasize that one of the real gains for them in working with student teachers is that these novices pose genuinely challenging questions and that, in either answering or, more often, thinking what the possible answers may be, the respondent is stimulated to reflect and so, in the way both Dewey and Schön have described, to reformulate. In a reflective cycle we are seeking to provide this kind of challenge *more consistently*. The teachers that I have worked with have never said, not surprisingly, that student teachers in themselves provide *sufficient challenge* for all their developmental needs. Teachers seek other stimuli: reading, subject associations, in-service courses, higher degrees and so on.

However, drawing on the notion of mentorship much more fully, as through the use of the departmental mentor and the mentoring stance, means that the stimulus to reflection becomes *more integrated* within daily professional life. Whatever the stage of the mentor–mentee (possibly mentees) relationship along the professional development continuum, we are essentially looking at certain reasonably common characteristics. These are some of characteristics of the reflective cycle in relation to the mentor–mentee relationship. These characteristics need thoughtful interpretation and contextualization. The pressures and tensions of school life are a constant force and, usually, obstructive to reflection and even conversation. In acknowledging these forces and their real power we are also recognizing how potentially dominating and limiting they are to professional and individual development. In the moments when genuine reflection takes place, something highly significant has been achieved and we need to strive against the pressures of school to create such moments.

Given the pressures, the following characteristics might be seen as somewhat ideal, but I do not consider them idealistic in its negative sense; that is, as impossible and unattainable. They are best viewed as features of professional conversations which, being of the best kind, are intelligent, thoughtful and purposeful and based on a genuine attempt at accurate empathy. In my view these conversations, over time, will tend to demonstrate:

- explicit and regular attention to an individual's development;
- explicit and regular attention to increasing an individual's awareness of 'where she is';
- emphasis on conversation and negotiation;
- respect for both partners of the other's position and needs;
- an attempt by both partners to achieve 'accurate empathy' but with the mentor recognizing she has the major role;

- an expectation that the mentor is enabled to learn through the conversation;
- a willingness on both sides to listen to experimental ideas and to express honest feelings of doubt as well as support;
- explicit attention to ways of evaluating any agreed actions.

In such ideal conversations there are great opportunities for mentee and mentor development. However, the main concern of the earlier sections of this book was to reveal the challenge of mentorship and to offer some insights into developing some expertise to rise to that challenge, especially as a subject mentor of English. Inevitably, such an 'ideal' conversation between a student teacher and her mentor will be likely to occur towards the end of a course, by which time that student may well have become not a highly accomplished teacher, but a highly accomplished student teacher.

Being a highly accomplished student teacher is, after all, no mean feat, just as being a highly accomplished mentor of student teachers is a very great achievement. At the end of the student's course that relationship will come to an end, even if the student gains a job in her host department, because new relationships need to be formed. The reflective cycle can continue but it will need to start from the relative positions of the new partners. At the conclusion of the mentor–student teacher relationship there is great scope for the celebration of what has been achieved. Helping someone along that continuum until she has become a highly accomplished student teacher of English is a tremendous achievement. In some cases simply bringing her as far as being competent is an equal achievement. I am emphasizing here that accomplishment is relative and that we need to celebrate its achievement at different stages.

If we acknowledge that gaining qualified teacher status is only a start to a valuable career, this does not detract from the quality of that start. If we are able to see it as a strong start to a continuum of professional development then this places that start within a properly developmental framework. At least some of that framework can be identified, potentially at least, as a part of the profession's infrastructure. The concept of mentorship, linked to the idea of a reflective cycle, offers positive ways forward for all concerned. The characteristics of the ideal conversation described above should be obtainable very consistently between peers when adopting the mentorship role.

The mentor and long-term quality development in schools

I should like to begin this conclusion with a few comments from mentors themselves. This is partly to give them, appropriately, some of the last words in a book for and about them, and to illustrate the range of feelings that being a mentor has inspired. The comments are not meant to be in a significant order but to provide some authentic voices from the mentors that I have worked with:

In many ways being a mentor has opened interesting dialogues with colleagues and with other involved teams (science, languages, art) and several initiatives have followed, e.g. the institution of informal/scheduled meeting of the heads of departments. I also feel that the role has had the effect of highlighting departmental practice re methodology – there is more discussion within the team, often to collect ideas on how to advise students.

It has been really good to be involved with training and guiding new teachers. It has made me more reflective about my own teaching.

I have always enjoyed acting as a mentor to students and to NQTs and now it is an even more important role – it is one area of responsibility that is truly rewarding and creative (I much prefer people to paper work).

I agreed to it originally for purely selfish reasons – it will look good on the CV. I am really enjoying it though. I found myself more and more involved. I read a lot of theory and this has helped me to feel equipped for the job, especially for answering difficult questions from students.

I have a real personal enthusiasm for the job and a long-term interest in it, and I think it fits very well with my desire to lead an outward-looking department.

I find students' development in terms of professional relationships (discussions about children, resources and teaching) is delightful to witness and a pleasure to be involved in.

There are many benefits, not least from their taking my classes. We all need more free lessons and my classes benefited from some excellent new ideas (and some brilliant wall displays).

Students develop when they are made to feel secure. Encouragement is the key issue – looking for strengths and gradually working on weaknesses. I think I am beginning to get the hang of that now.

I have been forced, not always comfortably, to reflect on my own practice and to develop it. I have had to be really explicit about my beliefs and to present them to an 'outsider'.

The whole partnership scheme has encouraged a high degree of personal reflectiveness, both as a teacher and as a manager. I have learned a lot about my own school because of having to work closely with the professional tutor. Contact with the university has been a good thing – breadth of vision and professional development.

I think I have learned how to focus their individual development. It is important to act as a regulator of the pace at which students learn – knowing *when* to provide *which* particular opportunities (and trying to ensure that our practice as a department is really consistent in key areas).

Meetings with other mentors have been excellent and have led to real improvements in the department.

The university days are lovely. The support in getting the partnership going has been excellent and thorough – sensitively planned and managed.

I want to continue in the role because I can develop and strengthen what I have already done. I feel my involvement enriches my understanding of English teaching and by exposure to the students' problems it helps me to be more sensitive to problems that other members of the department may be experiencing. I also value the link to the university as it provides an opportunity to learn something of current academic thinking.

I really think the role should stick with one person for a while because real expertise needs to be developed.

Ideally all teachers should undertake this role or a similar one because it changes your teaching and your understanding of professional relationships.

I would like to maintain the role for as long as possible since I derive so much personal and professional satisfaction from it. Of course, I accept that others could gain a lot from it but they will have to fight me for it and show that they are even keener than I am.

The whole experience has 'bonded' the department and given us a new common sense of purpose. We are beginning to speak the same language. The same applies with the university, where everything is gelling too. Basically a really strong bond is developing.

I still think the role needs more recognition in school, especially from the senior management team. I understand from last year's students that the head never spoke to any of them individually.

The role is intrinsically fulfilling, which is just as well. The headteacher just said 'professional development'. Isn't that what they always say when there's no money in it?

This is intentionally rather a collage of comments and, I hope, gives an airing to those real, individual voices. All these remarks about the mentorship role are in relation to student teachers. However, many of the comments are about the wide-ranging effects that have been apparent as a part of the move to school-based teacher education, and particularly because of the way the mentorship role acts as a catalyst. Inevitably, some of these 'effects' may diminish as school-based teacher education becomes more normal and more established, but, on the other hand, student teachers are, like the children, new every year. Some of the effects are going to be an ongoing element in the reflective cycle and current mentors clearly recognize and value them.

As I have tried to suggest, a reflective profession needs to look at the idea of a continuum of development across all schools, not just those that have chosen to host student teachers. Seen in this way, skilled mentorship can be a key element in helping to develop every English teacher. I have argued for mentorship to be seen as a role with generally consistent characteristics, but one that can be constantly adjusted to make the most of its potential. In this way it helps to make the most of the unconsciously incompetent student teacher and of the highly accomplished teacher alike. It does mean that we are seeking to build a different body of professional knowledge to complement our existing and developing expertise as teachers of children and adolescents. Creating and refining such a body of knowledge is both a long-term and an ongoing process. Reflective practitioners, of course, are critical, purposeful people. They rightly see 'bodies of knowledge' as potentially obstructive as well as useful and constructive. They always have their wits about them but they do not have all the answers.

I have always remembered a casual comment from a former colleague when I was still a very inexperienced teacher. He, the head of department, was remarking on a particular mistake that another inexperienced teacher had made with a class and on how resistant this teacher had been to advice. His final remark as he left the office was 'Still, I suppose you cannot short circuit someone's experience, can you?' I kept considering this phrase and still do. I took it to mean then that we have to experience most things in order, truly, to understand them, and that no one can really intervene in that process. I still think that is what he was trying to articulate and I know that I still ponder on this phrase because I believe so strongly in positive intervention. Why else would I have worked in education all these years? Yet it is true that we need experience in its powerful sense if we are to understand. However, there are some experiences that people should never have: some experiences damage and distort us. Fools and inexperienced teachers, given half a chance, really do rush in. How can we achieve the right balance between providing some experience and offering some wisdom?

There will never be a complete solution to this timeless problem, and any reflective professional will come to terms with the paradox. The reflective mentor is the kind of person and professional who nevertheless believes that positive intervention, however difficult, is worth the effort. She does want to offer some wisdom and find the best means of helping others to develop their own. In essence and in conclusion, good mentors make a difference to people's lives and excellent mentors make a huge and lasting difference.

Notes

Chapter 1

1 The history of teacher education is a field in itself, although not one extensively written about. Phil Gardner's (1993) chapter, The early history of school-based teacher training, is a useful and brief overview, as is Part 1 of Della Fish's excellent book (Fish, 1995).

2 The period of the 1960s and 1970s is the particular anxiety of a number of educational thinkers for a number of reasons. However, it is unquestionably a time when English was fundamentally changed from a principally Leavisite model to a more composite model including a much stronger language component. It is the period when real classroom research was under way and was revealing that many assumptions about teaching and learning needed rethinking; we are still in that process and need to accept that, once begun, that process is set to continue. A useful overview of these changes can be found in several chapters in Goodson and Medway (1990).

3 The term mentor comes from Homer's story of Ulysses. When Ulysses was going away he put Mentor in charge of everything, including his own son Telemachus. He wanted to ensure that Telemachus was not neglected but instead should be developed and educated by a close relationship with an appropriately experienced and caring role model. There is a long tradition, across cultures, of such positive and caring relationships, and there has been much renewed interest in this whole dimension of human activity in recent years. Caldwell and Carter (1993) provide a helpful overview of this trend aimed at a readership of professionals in education.

4 I am not aware of any major study of teachers' lore in the UK, but in the USA there was a funded project examining this issue and written up in Schubert and Ayers (1992). There is also a short, useful account of the project 'Teacher lore: learning about teaching from teachers', in a book with many interesting sections related to the education of English teachers (Shanahan, 1994).

5 This lack of training in relation to IT is not a problem solely for English; the whole teaching profession suffers from it to some extent. However, there are *particular problems* in relation to English teachers' views of where to place IT. Some people (I am one of them) are arguing for it to be placed within a broad conception of literacy, aligned with media education (see Goodwyn, 1992b), while others see it as a threat to a more traditional, print based view of literacy in which literature is the key

element. Recent, but as yet unpublished, research examining the attitudes of student teachers of English, their mentors and the views of teachers from their host departments suggests that the next generation of English teachers are likely to come into some conflict with currently established teachers over this issue. Some of these 'new' teachers are themselves far more skilled with IT and they are coming with a different view of its potential. To sum up, we face a difficult time when some teachers in senior positions may be unskilled and fundamentally resistant to the use of much IT in English, but able perhaps to thwart the initiatives of more skilled junior colleagues. The research in question was undertaken by Anthony Adams (Cambridge University), Stephen Clarke (Leeds University) and myself and sponsored by the National Council for Educational Technology.

Chapter 2

1 All the examples throughout the text and all the quotations are based on real people and their experiences. I have gathered this body of 'data' over the years through 'being there', through conversations with student teachers and teachers and through collecting evaluations and responses, again, from both student teachers and teachers. The names have all been changed.

2 In my view the best general book on mentoring, and one that has strongly influenced this book is Peter Tomlinson's superb *Understanding Mentoring* (1995). It is a thorough, comprehensive and extremely readable text. There are numerous others: I have quoted from several in the text and there are a number in the bibliography.

3 In terms of changes, I am really referring here to the various shifts of the National Curriculum, which are indeed innumerable and have affected every aspect of the English curriculum. However, English as a subject seems to me largely unchanged by these reorganizations. I believe that, deep down, English is changing, slowly, and will need to, to embrace the information and digital revolutions that now face us all. That is the subject for another book.

4 Some readers may be unfamiliar with the Language in the National Curriculum project and therefore may not know of this astonishingly blatant piece of political interference. The project was set up as a result of the Kingman Report (DES, 1988) which stressed the need for English teachers to have more knowledge about language in order to teach that component (knowledge about language) of the then emergent English National Curriculum. After three years of establishing the project, nationwide, costing £20,000,000 and creating an in-service network of advisers, the materials that were produced for teachers were effectively banned from schools at the last minute by the then Minister for Education.

5 Donald Schön has been one of the most influential thinkers in the field of professional practice. He has written many important contributions about the concept of the reflective practitioner. The best known are *The Reflective Practitioner: How Professionals Think in Action* (1983) and *Educating the Reflective Practitioner: towards a New Design for Teaching and Learning in the Professions* (1987). Much of Schön's work is indebted to John Dewey, arguably one of the most influential philosophers of this century. Of his numerous works, the most pertinent are *Democracy and Education* (1916), *The Quest for Certainty: a Study of the Relation of Knowledge and Action* (1929) and *Logic, the Theory of Inquiry* (1938).

Chapter 3

1 The discussion in Tomlinson's book (Tomlinson, 1995: Chapter 1) on mentoring provides a good review of the field and I would simply pick out the following two books as the best known recent additions to thinking about skill acquisition. David Kolb (1984) focuses especially on the idea of an experiential cycle; Dreyfus and Dreyfus (1986) have developed a five-stage model: (a) novice; (b) advanced beginner; (c) competent; (d) proficient; (e) expert.
2 An excellent starting point for further reading is Sally Brown and Donald McIntyre's (1993) *Making Sense of Teaching*, as are the collections (1993) and (1994) edited by McIntyre *et al.* (1993, 1994).

Chapter 4

1 Just in case it is not obvious, I am not a psychologist and I have drawn heavily on secondary sources for this book. I feel sure that for most readers there would be little point in my constantly citing these secondary sources.
2 This development in psychological theory dominates much of the twentieth century and has steadily influenced education. The key shift has been from a view of knowledge as something fairly static, and so to be accumulated, to a concept of knowledge as dynamic and as something that individuals create for themselves. The whole postmodern movement has struggled with this change, which is both liberating and destabilizing. Some of the implications for English are considered in Griffith (1991) and Green (1993). It is always reductive to simplify the work of important theorists, especially in a field in which one is an amateur. However, I have attempted to make use of the ideas of key theorists like Maslow and Rogers, as their work has become part of the intellectual infrastructure of a great deal of thinking in education. For readers of this book I would recommend a text like Medcof and Roth's (1979) *Approaches to Psychology* for a helpful overview. A more recent book, written directly for secondary teachers, *Secondary School Teaching and Educational Psychology* (Galloway and Edwards, 1992), is generally helpful, especially on Maslow's hierarchy of needs.

Chapter 5

1 There has been a steady movement, especially over the past twenty years, away from quantitative notions of research in education and other fields, and towards a qualitative approach. One key element in all this has been the recognition that we seem to understand the world and learn about it mostly through examples; these examples often come to us as anecdotes or complete stories. They might usefully be called, in professional dialogues, *cases*; that is, examples that help professionals to think about and reflect upon the nature of what they do and how they do it. Only some stories have this potential and professions tend to accumulate such stories as a professional body of knowledge; in medicine and law, cases are the very essence of professional knowledge. In teaching we seem to have begun the process, and I hope this book may convert more teachers to using cases as a means to professional development. A useful general book for all teachers is Stones (1992).

Chapter 6

1 Since the National Curriculum was first discussed in 1988 there have been various consultations and numerous changes to its content and some to the framework. Of all subjects, English has been the most conspicuous victim of ill-conceived and politically motivated 'changes'. For most of the changes there has technically been some form of consultation exercise. In each case the structuring of the response forms and the short time scale for returning opinions have meant that these exercises have been consultations in name only.

2 The collection edited by Grimmett and Erickson (1988) provides a very useful overview of Schön's work and offers a number of critical perspectives on his model of the reflective practitioner. Calderhead and Gates (1993) offers an in-depth look at how Schön's ideas work out when applied in differing professional situations.

3 I have already offered a few suggestions for further reading in relation to John Dewey's hugely influential work (see note 5 to Chapter 2). The only point to add here is that Dewey has had a tremendous, although indirect, influence on English teaching. The most obvious route is via Louise Rosenblatt, who uses Dewey directly in her work and whose development of reader response theory has steadily changed the nature of teaching about texts.

4 It is clearly far more than coincidental that there are moves under way in several developed countries to identify and certificate what might be called expert teachers. The most extensive schemes, to my knowledge, exist in the USA and Australia. The USA has created a National Board for Professional Teaching Standards, which is developing over fifty different certificates. At the time of writing the certificates are only just being implemented and it remains to be seen whether they will be taken up by the individual states themselves. The American certificates are extremely demanding and currently have a high 'failure' rate. In Australia the system is well established and is rather more low key. Each state has a quota of 'awards' and can recognize the achievement of a significant number of teachers each year, so that each school can perhaps identify at least one or two teachers each year. These teachers then receive a small pay reward.

5 ACE (The Advanced Certificate in the Teaching of English) is a collaborative research and development project involving Berkshire LEA and the University of Reading. It is coordinated by the Centre for Languages, English and Media Education at the University of Reading, funded by the university's 'Flexible learning project' and the Berkshire LEA/University of Reading Induction Project. Its aim is to develop a new certificate for expert teachers of English and subsequently for other subject teachers. The certificate will focus on classroom and school-based expertise and is designed to recognize and enhance the high-quality English teaching of participants. The certificate will be challenging and rigorous and will push highly accomplished English teachers to demonstrate their expertise in planning, teaching, assessing and working at the highest professional levels. It will be suitable both for those who manage, or wish to manage, English in schools and for those whose intention is to remain chiefly a classroom teacher. The research stage will continue over the years but the intense initial stage occupied January to July 1996. During this time a team made up from local schools, Berkshire LEA and the university met regularly to develop a trial version of the certificate and to prepare for the pilot phase. The team made full use of the resources of local schools, the

LEA and the university. The group's work is informed by existing research in teacher professional development and through the university's international links with the USA and Australia, countries in which there have been parallel developments.

Bibliography

Alexander, R.J., Craft, M. and Lynch, J. (eds) (1984) *Change in Teacher Education: Context and Provision since Robbins*, London: Holt, Rinehart and Wilson.

Argyris, C. and Schön, D. (1974) *Theory into Practice: Increasing Professional Effectiveness*, San Francisco: Jossey-Bass.

Berliner, D.C. (1986) In pursuit of the expert pedagogue, *Educational Reasearcher*, 15, 5–13.

Bernbaum, G., Patrick, H. and Reid, K. (1985) A history of post-graduate initial teacher education in England and Wales, 1880–1990. In D. Hopkins and K. Reid (eds) *Rethinking Teacher Education*, London: Croom Helm, pp. 7–18.

Bibby, B. and Wade, B. (1995) *English and the Ofsted Experience*, London: David Fulton Publishers.

Bridges, D. and Kerry, T. (eds) (1993) *Developing Teachers Professionally: Reflections for Initial and In-service Trainers*, London: Routledge.

Britton, J. (1970) *Language and Learning*, Harmondsworth: Penguin.

Brown, S. and McIntyre, D. (1993) *Making Sense of Teaching*, Buckingham: Open University Press.

Bruner, J.S. (1966) *Towards a Theory of Instruction*, New York: W.W. Norton.

Calderhead, J. (ed.) (1987) *Exploring Teacher Thinking*, London: Cassell.

Calderhead, J. and Gates, P. (eds) (1993) *Conceptualizing Reflection in Teacher Development*, London: Falmer Press.

Caldwell, B.J. and Carter, E.M.A. (eds) (1993) *The Return of the Mentor: Strategies for Workplace Learning*, London: Falmer Press.

CATE (1992) *The Accreditation of Initial Teacher Training under Circulars 9/92 (Department for Education) and 35/92 (Welsh Office)*, London: Council for the Accreditation of Teacher Education.

CATE (1993) *The Initial Training of Primary School Teachers: Circular 14/93 (England)*, London: Council for the Accreditation of Teacher Education.

Chi, M., Glaser, R. and Farr, M. (1988) *The Nature of Expertise*, Hillsdale, NJ: Lawrence Erlbaum Associates.

Cox, B. (1991) *Cox on Cox: an English Curriculum for the 1990s*, London: Hodder and Stoughton.

Cox, B. (1992) *The Great Betrayal: Memoirs of a Life in Education*, London: Chapmans.

Dart, L. and Drake, P. (1996) Subject perspectives in mentoring. In D. McIntyre and H. Hagger *Mentors in Schools: Developing the Profession of Teaching*, London: David Fulton.

Davies, C. (1996) *What is English Teaching?* Buckingham: Open University Press.

Day, C., Calderhead, J. and Denicolo, P. (eds) (1993) *Research on Teacher Thinking: Understanding Professional Development*, London: Falmer Press.

DES (1975) *A Language for Life* (the Bullock Report), London: HMSO.

DES (1988) *Report of the Committee of Inquiry into the Teaching of English Language*, London: HMSO.

DES (1989) *English for Ages 5 to 16*, London: HMSO.

Dewey, J. (1916) *Democracy and Education*, New York: Macmillan.

Dewey, J. (1929) *The Quest for Certainty: a Study of the Relation of Knowledge and Action*, New York: Minton, Balch.

Dewey, J. (1933) *How we Think: a Restatement of the Relation of Reflective Thinking to the Educative Process*, Chicago: D.C. Heath.

Dewey, J. (1938) *Logic, the Theory of Inquiry*, New York: Holt.

DFE (1992) Initial teacher training (secondary phase), Circular number 9/92, London: Department for Education.

DFE (1993a) The initial training of primary school teachers: new criteria for courses, Circular number 14/93, London: Department for Education.

DFE (1993b) *The Government's Proposals for the Reform of Initial Teacher Training*, London: Department for Education.

Dixon, J. (1967) *Growth through English*, 1st edn, Oxford: Oxford University Press.

Dreyfus, H.L. and Dreyfus, S.E. (1986) *Mind over Machine: the Power of Human Intuition and Expertise in the Era of the Computer*, New York: Macmillan.

Egan, G. (1990) *The Skilled Helper: a Systematic Approach to Effective Helping*, 4th edn, Pacific Grove, CA: Brooks/Cole.

Elliot, J. (1993) *Reconstructing Teacher Education: Teacher Development*, London: Falmer Press.

Field, B. and Field, T. (eds) (1994) *Teachers as Mentors: a Practical Guide*, London: Falmer Press.

Fish, D. (1989) *Learning through Practice in Initial Teacher Education*, London: Kogan Page.

Fish, D. (1995) *Quality Mentoring for Student Teachers: a Principled Approach to Practice*, London: David Fulton Publishers.

Galloway, D. and Edwards, A. (1992) *Secondary School Teaching and Educational Psychology*, Harlow: Longman.

Gardner, P. (1993) The early history of school-based teacher training. In D. McIntyre, H. Hagger and M. Wilkin (eds) *Mentoring: Perspectives on School-based Teacher Education*, London: Kogan Page.

Goodson, I. and Medway, P. (eds) (1990) *Bringing English to Order*, London: Falmer Press.

Goodwyn, A. (1992a) English teachers and the Cox models, *English in Education*, 28(3), 4–10.

Goodwyn, A. (1992b) *English Teaching and Media Education*, Buckingham: Open University Press.

Goodwyn, A. (ed.) (1995) *English and Ability*, London: David Fulton Publishers.

Green, B. (ed.) (1993) *The Insistence of the Letter: Literacy Studies and Curriculum Theorizing*, London: Falmer Press.

Griffith, P. (1991) *English at the Core: Dialogue and Power in English Teaching*, Buckingham: Open University Press.

Grimmett, P.P. and Erickson, G.L. (1988) *Reflection in Teacher Education*, Vancouver: University of British Columbia; New York: Teachers College Press.

Grossman, P. (1990) *The Making of a Teacher: Teacher Knowledge and Teacher Education*, New York: Teachers College Press.

Hagger, H., Burn, K. and McIntyre, D. (1993) *The School Mentor Handbook: Essential Skills and Strategies for Working with Student Teachers*, London: Kogan Page.

Hopkins, D. and Reid, K. (eds) (1985) *Rethinking Teacher Education*, London: Croom Helm.

Kaggan, D.M. (1992) Professional growth among pre-service and beginning teachers, *Review of Educational Research*, 62(2), 129–69.

Kelly, G.A. (1955) *The Psychology of Personal Constructs*, two volumes, New York: Norton.

Kolb, D.A. (1984) *Experiential Learning: Experience as the Source of Learning and Development*, Englewood Cliffs, NJ: Prentice Hall.

McIntyre, D., Hagger, H. and Wilkin, M. (eds) (1993) *Mentoring: Perspectives on School-based Teacher Education*, London: Kogan Page.

McIntyre, D., Hagger, H. and Burn, K. (1994) *The Management of Student Teachers' Learning: a Guide for Professional Tutors in Secondary Schools*, London: Kogan Page.

Mathieson, M. (1975) *The Preachers of Culture*, London: Allen and Unwin.

Medcof, J. and Roth, J. (1979) *Approaches to Psychology*, Milton Keynes: Open University Press.

Nelson-Jones, R. (1988) *Practical Counselling and Helping Skills: Helping Clients to Help Themselves*, 2nd edn, London: Cassell.

Olson, J. (1991) *Understanding Teaching: Beyond Expertise*, Buckingham: Open University Press.

Protherough, R. and Atkinson, J. (1991) *The Making of English Teachers*, Buckingham: Open University Press.

Rosenblatt, L. (1978) *The Reader, the Text, the Poem: the Transactional Theory of the Literary Work*, Carbondale, IL: Southern Illinois University Press.

Russell, T. and Munby, H. (eds) (1992) *Teachers and Teaching: from Classroom to Reflection*, London: The Falmer Press.

Saunders, S., Pettinger, K. and Tomlinson, P.D. (1995) Prospective mentor's views of school-based initial teacher education, *British Educational Research Journal*, 21, 2.

Schön, D.A. (1983) *The Reflective Practitioner: How Professionals Think in Action*, New York: Basic Books.

Schön, D.A. (1987) *Educating the Reflective Practitioner: towards a New Design for Teaching and Learning in the Professions*, San Francisco: Jossey-Bass.

Schubert, W.H. and Ayers, W.C. (eds) (1992) *Teacher Lore: Learning from Our Own Experience*, White Plains, NY: Longman.

Shanahan, T. (ed.) (1994) *Teachers Thinking, Teachers Knowing: Reflections on Literacy and Language Education*, Urbana, IL: The National Council of Teachers of English.

Shulman, L.S. (1986) Those who understand: knowledge growth in education, *Educational Researcher*, 15, 4–14.

Smith, P. and West-Burnham, J. (eds) (1993) *Mentoring in the Effective School*, Harlow: Longman.

Stones, E. (1984) *Supervision in Teacher Education: a Counselling and Pedagogical Approach*, London: Methuen.

Stones, E. (1992) *Quality Teaching: a Sample of Cases*, London: Routledge.

Tomlinson, P. (1995) *Understanding Mentoring: Reflective Strategies for School-based Teacher Preparation*, Buckingham: Open University Press.

Watkins, C. and Whalley, C. (1993) *Mentoring: Resources for School-based Development*, Harlow: Longman.

Wilkin, M. (ed.) (1992) *Mentoring in Schools*, London: Kogan Page.

Williams, A. (ed.) (1995) *Partnership in Secondary Initial Teacher Education*, London: David Fulton Publishers.

Winnicott, C. (1964) *Child Care and Social Work*, Welwyn, Herts: Codicote Press.

Wubbels, T. (1992) Taking account of student teacher's preconceptions, *Teaching and Teacher Education*, 2(3), 263–82.

Index

Alexander, R.J., 43–4
appraisal, 108–11

Barnes, D., 9
Benton, P., 32
Bernbaum, G., 7
Bibby, B., 112
Black Papers, the, 8
Boyson, R., 12
Britton, J., 8, 9, 95–7
Bruner, J., 128
Bullock Report, the, 8

Caldwell, B.J., 105
case studies, 99–105
Council for the Accreditation of
  Teacher Education (CATE), 9–11
Council for National Academic Awards
  (CNAA), 9
counselling, 3, 19, 73–90
Crowther, 8, 39

Day, L., 37–8
Desforges, C., 32, 38
Dewey, J., 43, 117–20
Dixon, J., 8

English teachers
  distinctive group, 29
  group work, 27–8, 57–8
  job interviews, 42
  models of English, 38–42, 71

professional development, 3, 25, 43,
  46, 115–34
reader response theory, 99–101
subject beliefs, 39–42, 71
subject pedagogical knowledge, 29–30,
  34
subject-selfishness, 61–2

Fish, D., 7
Freud, S., 73

Gardner, P., 7
Goodson, I., 9
Goodwyn, A., 38–9, 85, 93
Grimmet, P., 117
Grossman, P., 30–1

Her Majesty's Inspectors (HMI), 9–10

induction, 105
information technology, 24

Kelly, G., 73
Kingman Report, 34

Leavis, F.R., 9, 38

McIntyre, D., 43–5
Maslow, A., 73, 76, 101, 106
Mathieson, M., 29

newly qualified teachers, 99, 108–16

Ofsted, 111–14

Postgraduate Certificate in Education
   (PGCE)
  articled teachers, 10
  assessment, 3, 14, 19, 22, 91–8
  competence, 3, 14, 91–8
  external examiners, 18
  history of, 7–19
  interviews for, 1, 15–16, 18, 26, 29
  licensed teachers, 12
  mentors' own experience of, 6–7, 27
  national criteria, 13–14
  Open University, 10
  partnership models, 12–14
  professional tutors, 17
Protherough, R., 12, 29, 122, 129

reflective practice, 2, 3, 31, 33, 42–7, 53,
   58, 71, 116–21
Rogers, C., 73–4
Rosen, H., 9
Rosenblatt, L., 99

Schön, D., 43–7, 52, 54, 117–20
student teachers
  assessment of, 80–90, 91–8
  collaborative teaching, 65–6
  competence of, 51–2, 55–6, 81–90
  defensiveness of, 79–85
  evaluation, 54–5
  feedback to, 58–9

  formative influences upon, 28–35
  information technology, 24
  mature students, 78–9
  motivation of, 62–3
  observing, 27–8, 50, 58, 59–64
  orchestrating the learning of, 59
  planning, 54–5, 58
  professionalism, 20–1
  psychology of, 73–90
  reviewing, 56–8
  status of, 76–9
  stress on, 79–85
  subject beliefs, 38–42, 74, 98–9
  teaching attempts, 54–5, 65
  vocation, sense of, 19–20

Teacher Training Agency (TTA), 2,
   11
teaching
  collaborative, 65–6
  evaluation of, 54–5
  expertise, 53
  group work, 27–8, 57
  highly accomplished, 121–37
  knowledge-in-action, 52
  monitoring pupils, 58
  observation, 59–64
  planning, 54–5, 58
  reflection-in-action, 54, 104
Tomlinson, P., 54

Winnicott, C., 86–7